90 0699116 3

KV-478-281

Adult learning

at a glance 2006

the UK context, facts and figures

Veronica McGivney

Univ
Subjec

ht'

WITHDRAWN
FROM
UNIVERSITY OF PLYMOUTH

EUROPEAN UNION
European Social Fund

niace
promoting adult learning

Published by the National Institute of Adult Continuing Education
(England and Wales)

21 De Montfort Street
Leicester LE1 7GE
Company registration no. 2603322
Charity registration no. 1002775

Copyright © 2006 National Institute of Adult Continuing Education
(England and Wales)

All rights reserved. No reproduction, copy or transmission of
this publication may be made without the written permission of
the publishers, save in accordance with the provisions of the
Copyright, Designs and Patents Act 1988, or under the terms of
any licence permitting limited copying issued by the Copyright
Licensing Agency.

UNIVERSITY OF PLYMOUTH

9006991163

promoting adult learning

NIACE, the national organisation for adult learning, has a broad
remit to promote lifelong learning opportunities for adults. NIACE
works to develop increased participation in education and training,
particularly for those who do not have easy access because of
barriers of class, gender, age, race, language and culture, learning
difficulties and disabilities, or insufficient financial resources.

NIACE's website: www.niace.org.uk

Cataloguing in Publication Data
A CIP record of this title is available from the British Library

EUROPEAN UNION
European Social Fund

The production of this publication has been part-funded through the
European Social Fund.
The European Social Fund (ESF) is a European Union initiative to
promote employment opportunities for all. The ESF helps people
who need additional support to enter jobs, improve their skills and
develop their potential at work. For more information go to:
www.esf.gov.uk

ISBN 1 86201 269 5

Designed and typeset by Boldface, London.
Printed and bound by Latimer Trend, Plymouth.

Contents

Preface   ix
Acknowledgements   x

Pulling the threads together   1

    Improving qualification levels   2
    Persisting participation divides   2
    Part-time students   3
    Mismatch between policy and demographic realities   3
    Recruitment and training   4
    Policy priorities   4
    Sex differences   5

Section 1: Demography and lifestyle   7

1.1 Population trends   7
    Size   7
    Age profile   7
    Diversity   8
1.2 Asylum applications   8
1.3 UK Households   9
    Size   9
    Composition   9
1.4 Family and partnership patterns   9
1.5 Wealth and income   10
    Wealth   10
    Incomes   11
    Low incomes   12
1.6 Pensions   13
1.7 Debt   13
1.8 Social mobility   13
1.9 Measures to help those on low income or out of work   14
    In-work benefits   14
    Out-of-work benefits   15
1.10 Families on key benefits   16
    People over pension age   16
1.11 Household expenditure   16
    Prices   18
1.12 Housing and homelessness   18
    Homelessness   19
1.13 Health   19
1.14 Drug use   20
1.15 Social and civic participation   21
    Volunteering   22
    Civic participation   22
    Non-participation   22
1.16 Lifestyle and leisure   23
1.17 Ownership of and access to new technology   23
    Internet access   23
    Patterns of access and use   24
1.18 Crime and custody   25
    Prison population   26

Section 2: The labour market: occupational change, employment patterns and skill needs   27

2.1 Labour market and occupational trends   27
    Sector changes   27
    Differences in workers' occupational patterns   28
    Qualification level   28
    Sex   28
    Ethnic group   29
2.2 Employment and economic activity rates   29
    Regional variations   30
    EU comparisons   30
    Sex differences   31
    Age differences   32
    Qualification differences   33
    Employment patterns   34
    Part-time and temporary employment   34
    Self-employment   34
    Home working   35
    Economic activity rates   35
2.3 Unemployment/economic inactivity   36
    Long-term (2 years +) unemployed   36
    Unemployment rates by region   36
    Sex differences in economic inactivity and
      unemployment   37
    Age differences in economic inactivity and
      unemployment   37
    Workless households   37
    Factors involved in unemployment/economic inactivity   38
    Disadvantage   38
    Belonging to a minority ethnic group   38
    No or low qualification   39
    Sickness or disability   39
    Domestic and caring responsibilities   39
2.4 Earnings   40
    Earning differentials   40
    By sector   40
    By employee qualification level   40
    By sex   41
2.5 Benefit claimants   41
    Claimants of Jobcentre Plus benefits   41
    Regional differences   41
2.6 Government employment programmes:
    participation and results   42
    Changes to national programmes and initiatives for
      those not in work   42
    Pathways to Work   42
    Incapacity Benefit   42
    Pathways to Work for lone parents   43
2.7 Employment and Skill gaps   47
    Recruitment gaps   47

Skill shortages 48
Skills policies 49

Section 3: Educational attainment 50

3.1 International comparisons 50
3.2 Government policies and targets 50
3.3 Attainment of different qualifications 51
    GCSEs 51
    A-Levels or equivalent 51
    NVQs 51
    Full Vocational Awards 51
    Higher Education Qualifications 52
3.4 Highest Qualifications Held 52
3.5 Highest qualification by region 53
3.6 Level 2 achievement 53
3.7 Staying-on rates in England 55
3.8 Low or no qualifications 55
    Among the population as a whole 55
    Among young adults 55
3.9 Low levels of literacy, language and numeracy (LLN) 56
3.10 Sex differences in attainment 57
3.11 Subject variations 58

Section 4: Participation in post-compulsory education and training: rates and patterns 61

4.1 Post-16 participation rates 61
4.2 Regional variations 61
4.3 Participation in relation to ethnic background 64
4.4 Participation in relation to age 64
4.5 Participation in relation to sex 65
4.6 Participation in relation to terminal age of education 66
4.7 Participation in relation to level of qualification 67
4.8 Participation in relation to socio-economic status 67
4.9 Participation in relation to employment status 68
4.10 Participation related to income 69
4.11 Access to the Internet 69
4.12 Future intentions to learn 70
    Future intentions to learn, by age 70
    Future intentions to learn, by socio-economic status 70
    Future intentions to learn, by nation and region 71
4.13 Participation to gain qualifications 71

Section 5: Education sectors and provision 74

5.1 Higher Education (HE) 74
    Participation 74
    Type and level of study 74
    Higher National Diplomas (HNDs), Higher National Certificates (HNCs) and Foundation Degrees 75
    Part-time students 76
    Part-time students by subject area 77
    Motivations of part-time students 77
    HE students by domicile 78
    HE Students by age 79
    HE Students by sex 79
    HE students by ethnic background 81
    HE students by socio-economic background 82
    HE students by disability 82
    Open University (OU) student profile 82
    HE subject choice 84
    Variations in course choice 84

    Participation in science, engineering & technology 84
    Retention rates 84
    HE qualifications obtained 86
    Degree grades 87
    Destinations of full-time and part-time first degree graduates 87
    Full-time, first-degree graduates 87
    Employment 88
    Unemployment 88
    Part-time, first-degree graduates 88
    Destinations of other undergraduates 88
    Destinations of Foundation Degree graduates 88
    Destinations of postgraduates 88
    Destinations of students in teacher training 88
    Student support 89
5.2 Further education (FE) 89
    Participation in FE in the UK 89
    Participation in FE in England 90
    Participation in FE in Wales 92
    Participation in L SC-funded provision 92
    Characteristics of learners in FE 92
    Areas of study, 2003–04 97
    Sex differences in subject choice 97
    Adult and community learning 98
    Success rates in further education 98
    Retention rates 98
    Overall success rates 100
    Variations between student groups and course types 101
    Skills for Life (SfL) 106
    Progress towards the targets 106
5.3 Local Education Authority provision 106
    Participation 106
    Funding 106
    Curriculum 107
5.4 Learndirect 107
5.5 Programmes funded by the European Social Fund (ESF) 107

Section 6: Work-related education and training 108

6.1 Work-based learning (WBL) 108
6.2 Characteristics of WBL learners 109
6.3 Modern Apprenticeships 109
6.4 Entry to Employment (E2E) 109
6.5 Success rates in work-based learning 109
6.6 Government plans and priorities for work-based learning 115
6.7 Job-related training 115
6.8 Job-related training by country, region and area 115
6.9 Employer-provided training in England 116
6.10 Type and length of training received by group of employees 117
    Job-related training by trainee characteristics 117
6.11 Age and job-related training 121
6.12 Sex differences in job-related training 122
6.13 Vocational course choice: sex differences 123
6.14 Employer Training Pilots (ETP) 124
6.15 Training for unemployed people 124
    Jobcentre Plus provision 124

Section 7: Quality issues in provision for adults 125

7.1	Best providers of learning for adults	125
7.2	Characteristics of good learning provision	125
7.3	Poor providers in 2003–04	127
7.4	Weakest areas of learning	128
7.5	Areas of concern	128
7.6	Characteristics of the poorest providers	128
7.7	Inspectorate findings for different types of provider	128
	Adult and community learning	128
	Colleges	128
	Learndirect	128
	Prisons	128
	Work-based learning	129
7.8	Learner satisfaction	129

References 130

Notes 133

List of tables and figures

Table 1: Growth in numbers of people over 65, UK, 1994 to 2031　7

Table 2: People over 60 in selected advanced countries　7

Figure 1: Ethnic groups of Great Britain and their identity　8

Table 3: Asylum applications in 2003, EU　8

Table 4: Size of households 1971 and 2004, Great Britain　9

Table 5: People in households, by type of household and family, Great Britain　9

Table 6: Distribution of wealth, UK　10

Table 7: GDP per head, EU　10

Figure 2: Low income, by location, Great Britain　11

Figure 3: Median net individual income, Great Britain　11

Figure 4: Numbers on low incomes, Great Britain　12

Figure 5: Older people receiving benefits, Great Britain　13

Figure 6: Working households receiving Working and Child Tax Credits, Great Britain　14

Figure 7: Levels of income support for couples, UK　15

Figure 8: Working-age people receiving a key benefit for two years or more, Great Britain　15

Table 8: Household expenditure, UK　16

Table 9: Household expenditure, by socio-economic classification, UK　17

Figure 9: Change of consumer price index, UK　18

Table 10: Homelessness by household composition, England　19

Figure 10: Infant mortality rates by social class, Great Britain, 1993–2002　20

Table 11: Participation in community and voluntary activities, by highest qualification level　21

Table 12: Type of help given by formal volunteers, England and Wales, 2001 and 2003　22

Table 13: Participation in civic activities, England, 1986–2003　22

Table 14: Participation in sport or physical activity by age, Great Brain, 1987–2003　23

Figure 11: Households with access to the Internet, UK　23

Table 15: Purpose of Internet use by age, Great Britain　24

Table 16: Indictable offences, by sex and age, England and Wales　25

Table 17: Prisoners, by ethnic group, England and Wales　26

Figure 12: Occupational trends, UK, 1997–2004　27

Table 18: Jobs, by sex and industry, UK, 1984–2004　28

Table 19: Employment, by sex and occupation, UK　28

Table 20: Economic activity, UK, 1989 and 2004　29

Table 21: Employment rates, England　30

Table 22: Employment rates by sex, EU　32

Figure 13: Employment rates by sex, UK, 1971–2004　32

Table 23: Employment change by age, UK, 1997–2004　32

Table 24: Employment rate by sex and highest qualification, UK　33

Table 25: Flexible working patterns, UK　33

Table 26: Full and part-time employment by age, Great Britain　34

Figure 14: Self-employment by ethnic group, Great Britain　34

Figure 15: Economic activity rates by sex, UK, 1994–2004　35

Figure 16: Rates of unemployment and economic inactivity, UK, 1995–2004　36

Figure 17: Unemployment rates by region and nation, UK, 1993–2004　36

Figure 18: Unemployment by sex, UK, 1984–2004　37

Figure 19: Workless households, UK, 1998–2003　37

Table 27: Unemployment rates of disadvantaged groups, UK, 1994–2003　38

Figure 20: Inactivity rates by ethnic background, UK　38

Figure 21: Unemployed, by level of qualification, UK　39

Table 28: Reasons for economic inactivity by sex and age, UK　39

Figure 22: Earnings and highest qualification, UK　40

Figure 23: Pay and qualification by age, UK　40

Table 29: Highest and lowest paid occupations, Great Britain　41

Table 30: Adults depending on Jobcentre Plus benefits, Great Britain　41

Figure 24a: New Deal for Young People, UK, 1998–2005　42

Figure 24b: Young people into employment, UK, 1998–2004　42

Figure 25a: New Deal for Lone Parents, UK, 1998–2004　43

Figure 25b: Lone parents into employment, UK, 1998–2004　43

Figure 26a: New Deal for Long-Term Unemployed People 25+, UK, 1998–2004　44

Figure 26b: Long-term unemployed people aged 25+ into employment, UK, 1998–2004　44

Figure 27a: Employment Zones, UK, 2000–2004　44

Figure 27b: Employment Zones: participants into employment, aged 25+, UK, 2000–2004　44

Figure 28a: New Deal for Disabled People, UK, 2001–2004　45

Figure 28b: New Deal for Disabled People into employment, UK, 2002–2004　45

Figure 29: New Deal 50+, UK, 2003–2004　46

Figure 30a: Work-Based Learning for Adults, England, 2001–2004　46

Figure 30b: Work-Based Learning for Adults into Employment, England, 2001–2004　46

Figure 31: Productivity comparisons　47

Figure 32: Skills shortage, by sector, UK　47

Figure 33: Skills shortage, by occupation, UK　48

Figure 34: Skills in particularly short supply, UK　48

Figure 35: GCSE results, by region, England and Wales　51

Table 31: Highest qualification, by sex, age and ethnic
  origin, in UK   52
    Figure 36: High and low qualifications, by region
      and nation, UK, 2004   53
    Figure 37: At least NVQ Level 2 or equivalent by
      region, England   53
Table 32: Highest qualifications, by age and sex, Wales   54
Table 33: Qualifications, by age and by sex, Scotland   54
    Figure 38: No qualifications, by ethnic group and sex,
      Great Britain   55
    Figure 39: 19-year-olds with low or no qualifications,
      UK, 1996–2004   56
Table 34: Highest qualification, by age and sex,
  Great Britain   57
    Figure 40: Five or more GCSE grades A* to C/
      GNVQs, by sex and ethnic group, England   58
Table 35: GCSE or equivalent entries and achievements,
  by subject and sex, UK   58
Table 36: Qualifications attained by school leavers at
  SCQF Level 7, by subject and sex, Scotland   59
Table 37: A-level results of 16–18-year-olds, by sex,
  subject and grade   60
    Figure 41: Current or recent adult participation in
      learning, UK   61
Table 38: Adult participation in learning, by nation, UK   62
Table 39: Adult current or recent participation in
  learning, by region and nation, UK,   62
Table 40: Adult participation in any learning and taught
  learning, UK   63
Table 41: LSC-funded learners, by ethnic background,
  England   63
Table 42: Participation in learning by age, UK   64
Table 43: Current or recent participation in learning,
  by age, UK, 1996–2005   64
    Figure 42: Current or recent participation in adult
      learning, by sex, UK, 1996–2005   65
Table 44: Participation in learning, men and women
  compared, UK   65
Table 45: Participation in LSC-funded provision, by sex
  and ethnic background, England   66
Table 46: Adult participation in training and education
  by qualifications held, Scotland   67
Table 47: Adult participation in learning, by socio-
  economic class, UK, 1996–2005   67
Table 48: Current or recent adult participation in learning
  by employment status, UK, 1996–2005   68
Table 49: Benefit dependents reporting adult
  participation in learning, UK   69
    Figure 43: Future intentions to learn by learning
      status, UK   70
Table 50: Future intentions to learn, by age, UK   70
Table 51: Future intentions to learn, by socio-economic
  class, UK   71
Table 52: Future intentions to learn, by region and
  nation, UK   71
Table: 53: Qualifications worked towards, by student
  profile, UK   72
Table 54: Number of FE and HE establishments, UK   74
    Figure 44: All HE students by level and mode of
      study, UK   75

Table 55: First-year students studying for FDs, HNDs and
  HNCs in different subject areas, UK, 2002–03 and
  2003–04   75
Table 56: Part-time students by subject area, mode,
  sex and non-UK domicile, UK   77
Table 57a: Non-EU European students by country of
  domicile, UK   78
Table 57b: Non-EU by country of domicile outside Europe
  (top 10), UK   78
Table 58a: Age of first-year undergraduates, by mode of
  study, UK   79
Table 58b: Age of first-year postgraduates, by mode of
  study, UK   79
Table 59: All HE students, by sex, mode and
  domicile, UK   80
Table 60: Ethnic minority students as a percentage, UK   81
    Figure 45: Female undergraduates, by known ethnic
      group and mode of study, UK   81
Table 61: First-year HE students, by qualification aim,
  mode of study and disability, UK   83
Table 62: Percentages of all students, by subject area,
  level and mode of study, UK   85
Table 63: HE qualifications, by level of qualification,
  mode of study and domicile, UK   86
    Figure 46: Degree classification, by sex, domicile and
      mode, UK   87
Table 64: First or upper second class honours degrees, by
  subject, UK   87
Table 65a: FE learners, by mode of study, sex and
  area of learning, UK   89
Table 65b: Of which overseas students   90
    Figure 47: FE learner numbers, England, 1996–2004   91
Table 66: FE learners, by type of college, England   91
Table 67: FE learners, by age and mode of study, England   91
Table 68: FE learners, by level, England   92
Table 69: FE learners, by institution type, mode of
  attendance and age, England, 2003 and 2004   93
Table 70: FE learners, by age, mode of attendance and
  sex, England, 2003 and 2004   94
Table 71: FE learners, by ethnicity and sex, England,
  2003 and 2004   95
    Figure 48: FE areas of study, England   97
Table 72: FE learners, by age and sex, England   98
Table 73: Learners in ACL, by ethnicity and sex, England,
  2003 and 2004   98
Table 74: Retention rates, by age group and length of
  qualification, England   99
Table 75: Retention rates by institution type, age group
  and qualification length, England   99
    Figure 49: FE college success rates, England
      1997–2003   100
Table 76: Success rate of full Level 2 qualifications,
  England   100
Table 77: Success rates, by institution type, age group,
  qualification length and expected end year, England   102
Table 78: FE success rates, by area of learning, qualification
  length and expected end year, England, 2001–2004   103
Table 79: FE success rates, by area of learning, sex and
  expected end year, England, 2001–2004   104
Table 80: FE success rates, by ethnicity, sex and
  expected end year, England   105

Table 81: FE success rates, by disability, sex and
   expected end year, England   105
Table 82: Starts in LSC-funded work-based learning, by
   age group and programme type, England, 2003–04   108
Table 83: Success rates in work-based learning, by age
   group and programme type, England   110
Table 84 Success rates in work-based learning, by area of
   learning, sex and programme type, England   111
Table 85: Success rates in work-based learning, by
   ethnicity and programme type, England   114
Table: 86: Adult participation in education and training,
   by age, Scotland   115
Table 87: Employees and self-employed who received job-
   related training, by region and nation and by highest
   and lowest unitary authorities/local authority districts,
   Great Britain   116
Table 88: Employees receiving job-related training in
   previous four weeks, England   116
Table 89: Participation in job-related training in the
   previous four weeks, by type of training and economic
   characteristics, UK   118
Table 90: Participation in job-related training in the
   previous four weeks, by economic activity and age, UK 119
Table 91: Participation in job-related training in the
   previous four weeks, by type of training and a range of
   personal characteristics, UK   120
Table 92: Workers receiving job-related training in
   the previous three months, Scotland   121
      Figure 50: Employees offered and/or receiving
         education or training in the previous 13 weeks,
         Great Britain   121
Table 93: Duration of training period, Great Britain   122
Table 94: Workers receiving training in the previous
   13 weeks, by sex and age, Great Britain   122
      Figure 51: Employees receiving job-related training
         in the previous four weeks, by sex and age, UK   122
Table 95: Modern Apprenticeships, by sex, England   123
Table 96: Best ACL providers, by category, England 125
Table 97: Top ACL providers, England   126
Table 98: Poor ACL providers, England   127

Preface

This is the second edition of *Adult Learning at a Glance* – a digest intended to provide background facts and figures for those working with or doing research into issues related to adult learners.

Post-16 education and training do not exist in a vacuum. The services offered and their take-up are connected with and affected by a range of factors including demographic change, economic and labour market trends and policy measures. It is important when looking at post-compulsory education and training, therefore, to have an overview of what is happening in the population as a whole.

As in the first edition, the volume covers three main topic areas:

- The UK population (demographic trends, size and types of households, income levels, lifestyles, time use, cultural, social and civic engagement).
- The labour market (economic trends, skill needs, employment and unemployment).
- Education and training (educational attainment, participation in different post-16 education and training sectors).

There is also an additional short section on quality issues in adult learning.

The data are taken from official sources such as the Office of National Statistics, different government departments, recent Labour Force Surveys, the Learning and Skills Council, the Higher Education Statistics Agency and statistics sections of the Welsh Assembly and the Scottish Executive, and from charity websites, research publications and NIACE's own material.

It should be noted that consistent data are not available for all parts of the UK and that sometimes it has not been possible to obtain up-to date figures for all the items covered in this volume.

All sources are detailed at the end of the book.

Acknowledgements

I am very grateful to Marina (Scottish Assembly) and Susan Full (National Assembly for Wales) for their help with regional data; to Ozan Jaquette (formerly of Oxford University) for sharing her analysis of ILR; and Becci Newton (Institute for Employment Studies) for permission to quote from their report in training older workers. I am particularly grateful to Andy Kail and Anita Curtis for their invaluable help with information sources and to Sue Parkins for all her help throughout the compilation of this document

Pulling the threads together

A principal aim of *Adult Learning at a Glance* is to provide contextual data that enable links and connections to be made between post-compulsory education and training and other areas and dimensions of life in the UK. Experience of education, its relevance and impact, are influenced by a whole range of social, cultural and economic factors as well as by characteristics such as age, family background, social class and income, ethnicity, state of health and disability. Looking across the different sections of this volume, it is possible to see statistical links between many of these factors and levels of educational attainment, and between levels of educational attainment and participation in post-compulsory education and the labour market.

Changes in population trends, social mores and economic and employment patterns all have implications for post-compulsory education and training provision, and patterns of participation in them. The data included here show that there is, for example, a clear connection between social and economic inequalities and educational inequalities. Although there has been a number of positive measures to help those on low incomes (the minimum wage, working people's tax credits, Council Tax benefit, fuel payments for the elderly), Section 1 indicates that poverty is still a persisting feature of British society and that people have great difficulty extricating themselves from it. Research cited in Section 1 has found that social mobility in Britain is lower than in many other developed and affluent countries. Massive rises in housing costs, considered (inexplicably in the view of this writer) a sign of economic health, have strongly reinforced economic and social divisions. They have had knock-on effects for wages and salaries with resulting job losses (as companies contract services out to countries with lower labour costs); for cash-strapped local councils (the number of homeless families in temporary accommodation has increased by 123 per cent since 1997), and for social and health services which have to deal with the consequences of homelessness for families and individuals. An additional irony is that such services are often inadequately staffed, as many of those working in essential public sector jobs are themselves priced out of the housing market (a quarter of all those earning less than £6.50 per hour are directly employed by the public sector).

Many adults in the poorest fifth of the population have a limiting long-standing illness or disability, twice the rate for those on average incomes. They are also the least likely to engage in community or civic activity and the least likely to possess personal computers and to have access to the Internet. Surveys repeatedly show that this 'digital divide' reflects and reinforces the learning divide between those who participate in organised education and training and those who do not.

The data presented in the following sections show that poverty and social class have a direct impact on learning achievement and that levels of learning achievement impact in their turn upon living standards, health, employment and income, creating a vicious circle that is difficult to break Early disadvantage impedes learning attainment, and gaps in progress between children from different socio-economic backgrounds tend to widen as they move through the formal education system. According to research cited in Section 1, the fact that social mobility in Britain is lower than in many other developed countries can in part be attributed to the relationship between poverty and low educational attainment. The sections on demography and employment demonstrate the severity of the subsequent impact of low educational attainment on different areas of life.

- Those with low or no qualifications are more likely to be in debt, to live in temporary or rented accommodation, to have poorest health and lowest life expectancy.

- Young men aged between 17 and 30 with no qualifications are nearly three times as likely to commit a serious offence as those with some qualifications.

- Although overall employment rates are higher than they have been for some years, those without qualifications are about 25 per cent more likely to be unemployed than those with a Level 2 qualification, and 30–40 per cent more likely to be unemployed than those qualified to Levels 3 or 4. Those who are employed often earn extremely low wages. Half of all 24- to 29-year-old employees with no qualifications earn less than £200 per week.

Section 2 shows that the level of qualification is generally reflected in the level of jobs held. In Spring 2004, 91 per cent of employees in professional occupations and 65 per cent of managers and senior officials held two or more A-levels or a higher-level qualification, compared with 22 per cent of process, plant and machine operatives and 21 per cent of those in elementary occupations – groups who are among the least likely to engage in post-16 education. However, the equation is not true for all ethnic groups. While Section 4 shows that ethnic minorities are more likely than white groups to seek qualifications, the data in Section 2 indicate that people of Bangladeshi, African, Pakistani and Caribbean descent are twice as likely as white people to be out of work but wanting work.

Improving qualification levels

The good news, as shown in Sections 3 and 5, is that overall qualification levels have risen substantially since the early 1990s. Success rates in post-compulsory education and training sectors, especially further education, have increased significantly in recent years and continue to rise. The UK is now ranked above the OECD average in relation to the proportion of the workforce qualified to NVQ Level 4 and above, and it has one of the highest rates of university graduation in the 30 OECD countries. In spring 2004, 45 per cent of people of working age in the UK were qualified to Level 3 equivalent or above, and 26 per cent to Level 4 equivalent or above. Alongside this, however, almost 30 per cent of all 19-year-olds lacked a Level 2 or equivalent and one in twelve had no qualifications at all, the same proportion as in 2000. Overall, about 15 per cent of people of working age in the UK still have no qualifications.

This is a situation that the government is understandably anxious to reverse. Accordingly, the main thrust of post-16 education policy is to increase qualification levels. Qualifications are seen as a proxy for skills and a means of improving the country's economic competitiveness, raising living standards and improving social and civic participation. Major current strategies to achieve this goal are the commitment to offer adults free 'Skills for Life' (literacy, language and numeracy) and free learning up to a full Level 2 for adults who do not have that level of qualification. The latter measure is designed to meet the public sector agreement target of reducing the number of economically active adults who lack a Level 2 or equivalent by the year 2110. Will this strategy succeed? The data presented in Section 4 give some cause for doubt.

Persisting participation divides

Despite a plethora of initiatives since the 1990s designed to widen participation in learning, the NIACE participation surveys have found that the overall number of adult learners, especially those in the most educationally disadvantaged categories, has not grown significantly since 1996. Although government surveys generally extrapolate a higher number of learners than the NIACE surveys, they also show a drop in the number of people reporting recent learning compared with 2002–03 (Section 4). Like all its predecessors, the NIACE 2005 survey (Aldridge and Tuckett, 2005) found that professional and managerial groups are still about twice as likely to participate in learning as unskilled groups. While there has been an increase in the participation of skilled workers (C2s) over the last decade, only about one in four of unskilled and unwaged people claim to have engaged in learning in recent years, a situation that remains stubbornly resistant to change. Major strategies to widen participation in learning such as the ill-fated Individual Learning Accounts of a few years ago, and measures to widen access to higher education, have chiefly benefited those from more affluent backgrounds. Longitudinal research indicates that university graduation rates from the poorest fifth of families have increased from 6 per cent to 9 per cent, but have risen from 20 per cent to 47 per cent for the richest fifth (Blanden et al, 2005). Moreover, the Griffiths (2005) Commission on Personal Debt cited in Section 1, refers to student loans as 'a growing problem' that is likely to worsen as a result of rising tuition fees and living expenses. This prospect may well deter those from lower income groups from contemplating higher education, although many universities are developing bursary and other schemes to attract them.

Educational inequalities therefore persist. This shows up clearly in the case of part-time students.

Part-time students

The data presented in Sections 4 and 5 show that although most adult learners in further education and a growing number in higher education are studying part-time, public funding and other support mechanisms are far lower for part-time learners than for those studying full-time. In higher education, part-time students now represent about 42 per cent of all students. Over 70 per cent of these are aged over 30. Despite this, part-time HE students are routinely ignored in policy and were omitted from discussion in the 2004 Higher Education Act. They are also discriminated against as they are obliged to pay fees upfront and are not entitled to the bursaries available to full-time students. The imposition of top-up fees in 2006 could therefore lead to a significant reduction in part-time enrolments, which could have a particularly negative impact on institutions such as Birkbeck and the Open University and other higher education institutions that attract a high number of mature part-time students. Research cited in Section 4, showing that the majority of part-time students in higher education are studying for employment-

related reasons – i.e. reflecting government priorities – makes this situation illogical as well as grossly inequitable.

Other forms of educational inequality also persist. The Adult Learning Inspectorate (quoted in Section 7) has found that post-16 education providers do not adequately cater for some groups with the lowest attainment levels. In his annual report for 2004, the Chief Inspector forcefully expressed his dissatisfaction at the standards of provision for people with learning difficulties or disabilities, those who gained no or few qualifications at school and offenders (ALI, 2004).

Many of those working in the adult education field are also worried by the neglect of older learners in post compulsory policy and provision. In relation to this group, comparison of data in Sections 1, 2, 4 and 6 reveals a worrying lack of coordination between policy priorities and social and economic realities.

Mismatch between policy and demographic realities

The demographic data and forecasts reproduced in Section 1 indicate that people over pensionable age in the UK currently make up about 18 per cent of the population and that in just a few decades, this proportion will grow to 25 per cent, with only about half the population aged under 45. The implications for the labour market and for health, social and welfare services, are profound.

The economy in particular will be affected since, in future years, there will be insufficient numbers of young people entering the UK labour market to fill all the new and replacement jobs needed. It is estimated that two-thirds of vacancies will therefore need to be filled by other groups including older adults, those outside the labour market (such as non-working women), people on welfare benefits and immigrants. To integrate these different groups into the labour market will require tailored strategies, some of which, such as the New Deals, are already in train, and changes to Incapacity Benefit.

The Department of Work and Pensions (DWP,

2005a) aspires to achieve an overall employment rate of 80 per cent, The targets identified include getting one million people off Incapacity Benefit and bringing 0.3 million more single parents and one million people aged over 50 into employment.

Prolonging working life is another of the options being considered for filling gaps in the labour market and alleviating what is often described as the pensions crisis. Although there are more older people in employment now than there were a few years ago, the data set out in Section 2 indicate that the proportion of full-time employees declines for those aged 55 and over and then sharply for those over 60. For people over the state pension age, economic activity rates are 9 per cent for men aged 65 and over, and 10 per cent for women aged 60 and over. This is not always a matter of choice. There has long been evidence of employer prejudice against recruiting and retaining older workers.

Recruitment and training

The skills and labour market data presented in Section 2 highlight some of the contradictions in employer recruitment practices. Many employers responding to the National Employers' Skills Surveys (Hogarth *et al*, 2004) report that the skills of their workforce are not sufficient, and that vacancies remain unfilled due to shortages of ICT skills, technical and practical skills, sales and customer service skills, communication and information-handling skills.

The survey of employer recruitment and retention cited in Section 2 (CPID, 2004) found that 85 per cent of firms had experienced difficulty in recruiting staff over the previous year, and 45 per cent reported that the most difficult vacancies to fill were management and professional vacancies. Yet, according to the Third Age Employment Network:

A 50+ manager or professional out of the labour market will find it next to impossible to return at a level similar to their last job. {We} hear from such people every week. There is still much to understand about management planning and attitudes to age (TAEN, 2005a).

The Network comments on the 'conundrum' that

labour and skills shortages coexist with large pools of non-working people, especially in major cities. This situation, coupled with demographic changes suggesting that older workers will be crucial to the economy in coming years, highlights the need for fundamental changes in employer attitudes and practices. Appointing workers over 50 and developing the current workforce rather than recruiting new staff could be effective means of combating skills shortages. Older workers returning to the labour market will need training, while those who are extending their working life will need regular upskilling. However, the Labour Force Surveys invariably show a sharp decline in the training received by those aged over 50. Many employers, as demonstrated by the data in Section 6, offer little or no training to their older workers, and what training is offered is usually on the job and of short duration. This neglect can be seen as part of a general pattern. The need to develop older workers' skills was ignored in the Skills Strategy (DfES, 2003a), in which older people figure only as 'pensioners' – with all the connotations of economic inactivity that the term implies. Moreover, few Local Learning and Skills Councils or Regional Development Agencies pay any explicit attention to older learners. Post-16 educational policy as a whole attaches far greater priority to those aged 14–19, with funding subsidies for the education and training of this cohort considerably more than those made available for those aged 19+.

Not only is this inequitable: it is also illogical as it contradicts the government's own aspirations and other departmental priorities. The DfES and DWP appear to be singing from different song sheets. Given the implications of demographic changes outlined in Section 1 and the economic need to recruit, retain and (re)train older workers, the over-riding priority attached to education and training for those aged 14–19 is difficult to comprehend.

Policy priorities

Reflecting overall education policy as set out in the Skills Strategy, the LSC's (2004a) stated priorities for 2005–06 are to:

- Make learning truly demand led.

- Ensure that all 14–19 year-olds have access to quality learning.
- Transform further education so that it attracts business investment in skills training.
- Strengthen (the LSC's) role in regional regeneration.
- Extend (LSC) influence on economic development and job creation.
- Improve the skills of workers in the public sector.

The reduction in public funding support for adult learning that is not explicitly related to these priorities puts the government's Level 2 target at risk as it could (and probably will) result in a further reduction in adult participation in learning. Data included in Section 1 indicate that the costs of education have risen more than those of other selected goods and services in the past few years, and that people spend far less on education than on other areas of expenditure. Two large occupational groups (intermediate, routine and manual workers) spend less on education and participate less than other groups. At a time when fee levels for courses and programmes that are not linked to government priorities are rising, this has clear implications for future levels of adult participation. It is likely that people in these occupational categories (and others on low incomes) who are not ready or willing to enter a process leading to a full Level 2, may find it difficult to access less formal and non-accredited learning opportunities that interest them and which they can afford. Yet, as the NIACE 2005 survey states:

Demographic change and government's own targets suggest that attracting adults into learning is essential and not only those without a full Level 2 (...)
There are challenging times ahead both for local authority ACL services and for FE provision as LSC budgets tighten and become aligned more closely with LSC priorities. A new funding system is promised and no one yet knows the impact (Aldridge and Tuckett, 2005).

Adult and community learning (ACL) – the area of learning that gets the highest approval ratings in the LSC Student Satisfaction survey (LSC, 2004b) – is excluded from the LSC priorities listed above, despite the fact that it has been a major element of provision in general further education colleges for

some years and although in his annual report for 2004, the Chief Inspector described it as 'a vital part' of the learning and skills sector, with a central part to play in securing its inclusiveness and relevance to real need (ALI, 2004).

Some of the main skills shortages identified in the National Employers' Skills Surveys (sales and customer service skills, communication and information-handling skills) are ones that ACL has a key role in developing, given its proven record (shown in the work of the DfES-funded Centre for Research in the Wider Benefits of learning) of promoting confidence, communication and social skills and tolerance towards others. Research undertaken by the Centre, some of it based on the longitudinal cohort studies being conducted at the University of London, has also provided quantifiable evidence of the invaluable contribution that ACL can make to health, well-being and social cohesion.

Women will bear the brunt of any future funding reductions since they are the majority of learners in ACL. As women also constitute the majority of part-time learners in both further and higher education, they are also most affected by the continuing policy neglect and lack of support for this group of learners.

Sex differences

Curiously, most surveys of adult learning participation find that more men are learning overall than women. This is at odds with other participation data, which show that women predominate in all forms of post-16 provision except work-based learning (although even here they tend to engage in more employer-provided training than men). It is possible that men are more likely to report (and in some cases talk up?) their learning than women, and in particular that they are more likely than women to report non-organised forms of learning such as self-directed learning.

Surveys also find that men have higher qualifications than women overall. This is due to an age cohort factor as there are more older women in the population without qualifications than men. However, the speed with which women are overtaking men at all levels of educational attainment (see Section 3) suggests that this feature could be reversed in a few years.

Despite women's increasing levels of attainment, and despite legislation to combat inequality, there are still unacceptable employment and earning differentials between men and women. Contradicting recent well-publicised complaints from (some) men that women are taking over the world, Sections 1 and 2 demonstrate clearly that women have considerably lower incomes than men at all stages of the life cycle, and earn less than men in most occupational categories. Some groups – those with dependent children, part-time workers and women of pension age – are particularly financially disadvantaged in relation to their male counterparts.

Section 2 shows that women are still concentrated in the lower-paid (often part-time) jobs and sectors and at the lower staffing levels, despite the fact that from early years onwards, they achieve higher success rates than men at all levels of formal education. Part of the reason for this is persisting sex stereotyping in educational and occupational choices. In 2003–04, women held 91 per cent of apprenticeships in Health, social care and public services but only 3 per cent in Engineering and 1 per cent in Construction. These patterns of learning have a direct impact on women's future employment and earnings potential, for public sector jobs are low paid by comparison with those in the private sector. Women's choices can be attributed partly to social and cultural conditioning but also, as the analysis of calls to the Learndirect learning advice line summarised in Section 5 suggests (Learndirect, 2004), to their characteristic motivations in relation to employment (although these themselves could also be the result of social conditioning).

The Learndirect analysis revealed that women making enquiries about learning and occupational oppor-tunities are primarily motivated by job satisfaction and doing something 'socially useful'. Men are motivated more by earning potential. This is reflected in the move away from interest in IT (a popular and potentially lucrative career choice just a couple of years ago) towards training for industries that offer relatively high rates of pay due to skills shortages – plumbing, electrical installation and plastering. The

analysis describes this as a 'massive trend'.

These and other cross-connections between demographic, labour market and education data place the latter firmly in the wider context. They suggest that judgments and measures relating to adult learning provision and participation should not be arrived at without reference to the economic and social circumstances and conditions that create or deny people the possibility of engaging in learning. Any national strategies to increase adult participation and attainment levels need to take these other factors into account.

There are also particular issues and questions arising from the education and training data that need to be addressed, notably:

- Why, given all the signs of their increased presence in the population and their importance to the future economy, does the education and training of older adults remain such a neglected issue?

- Given the singular lack of success of recent measures in increasing participation in learning among the most educationally disadvantaged groups, how will the raising of fee levels for less formal, non-accredited learning but the offering free learning for formal accredited learning – a process that so many people fear and shun – achieve greater participation?

- Why, given their growing numbers in further and higher education, is there not more financial and other support for part-time students?

- Given the push to increase qualification levels in the population, what measures are being taken to adequately prepare and support mature students in higher education when it is clear that they withdraw in greater numbers than younger students in their first year?

- Why are so few members of ethnic minority communities joining the Apprenticeship scheme?

Inequalities in education reflect inequalities in other areas of life and vice versa. Attempts to combat them in one context should have positive spin-offs in the others. The vicious circle needs to be broken.

Section 1

Demography and lifestyle

Most of the tables, figures and charts below are taken from Babb, Martin and Haezewindt (eds) (2004) *Focus on Social Inequalities* 2004 edition, ONS; *Social Trends 2005*, and the poverty.com website.

1.1 Population trends

Size

In 2003:

- There were 59.6 million people living in the United Kingdom
- Wales gained 15,000 people from net migration within the UK and Scotland gained 13,000 people. England experienced a net loss of 28,000 people.
- An estimated 151,000 more people arrived to live in the United Kingdom for at least a year than left to live elsewhere.

Age profile

- Between 1971 and 2003 the number of people in the UK aged 65 and over rose by 28 per cent, while the number of those aged under 16 fell by 18 per cent.
- The proportion of people in the UK aged 85 and over increased from 0.7 per cent in 1961 to 1.9 per cent in 2002.
- In 2004, there were 10.8 million people in the UK over pensionable age – 18 per cent of the population. In 2020, 1 in 4 of the UK population (25 per cent) is anticipated to be 60-plus. By 2021 pensioners will make up about 20 per cent of the population and by 2040 25 per cent, with only about half the population aged under 45 (Table 1).

The changing demography of the UK is similar to that of other developed countries such as France,

Table 1: **Growth in numbers of people over 65, United Kingdom, 1994–2031**

Age	1994	2001	2011[a]	2021[a]	2031[a]
All 65-plus (millions)	9.2	9.3	10.0	11.7	14.0
Percentage of population	*15.7*	*15.5*	*16.4*	*19.2*	*23.2*
All 75-plus (millions)	4.0	4.4	4.5	5.2	6.4
Percentage of population	*7.0*	*7.4*	*7.5*	*8.5*	*10.6*
All 85-plus (millions)	1.0	1.2	1.3	1.4	1.8
Percentage of population	*1.7*	*2.0*	*2.1*	*2.3*	*2.9*

a Projections

Source: BGOP, 2000, chapter 1; cited in Schuller, 2005.

Table 2: **People over 60 in selected advanced countries as a percentage of the total population, 1990–2040**

	1990	2000	2010[a]	2020[a]	2030[a]	2040[a]
France	18.9	20.2	23.1	26.8	30.1	31.2
Germany	20.3	23.7	26.5	30.3	35.3	32.5
Italy	20.6	24.2	27.4	30.6	35.9	36.5
Japan	17.3	22.7	29.0	31.4	33.0	34.4
UK	20.8	20.7	23.0	25.5	29.6	29.5
USA	16.6	16.5	19.2	24.5	28.2	28.9

a Projections

Sources: Merrill Lynch; Watson Wyatt, *FT* Survey 10 November 2000, cited in Schuller, 2005.

Germany, Italy and Japan, where on average about 20 per cent of the population are now aged 60 years or over. By 2050, this is expected to rise to 32 per cent (Table 2).

On the other hand there were 696,000 live births in the UK in 2003 – the largest single-year change since 1979 and the highest number since 1999.

Diversity

The size of the minority ethnic population in the UK is about 4.6 million – nearly 8 per cent of the total population. Half of the ethnic minority population is Asian (mainly Indian, Pakistani or Bangladeshi), and a quarter describe themselves as black, either African or Caribbean. (*Social Trends*, 2005).

1.2 Asylum applications

In 2003, France and UK had the highest number of applications for asylum (excluding dependants) of the then 15 members of the EU (Table 3). That year, applications to the UK fell by 41 per cent to 49,405.

The nationalities accounting for most applicants to the UK were Somali, Iraqi, Chinese, Zimbabwean and Iranian.

An estimated 28 per cent of applications to the UK in 2003 resulted in permission to remain being given: grants of asylum 5 per cent, of exceptional leave to remain, humanitarian protection or discretionary leave 11 per cent, allowed appeals 12 per cent.

Asylum removals (including assisted returns and voluntary departures) rose by 21 per cent in 2003. That year 29 per cent more failed asylum seekers were removed than in 2002 (Home Office, 2004).

The fall in applications was repeated in 2004 when asylum requests were down by 33 per cent in Britain. This compares with a drop of 30 per cent in Germany and 25 per cent in Sweden. France, where applications rose, remained the most popular destinations for asylum-seekers.

Figure 1: **Proportion of ethnic groups of Great Britain who consider their identity to be British, English, Scottish or Welsh, 2002–03**

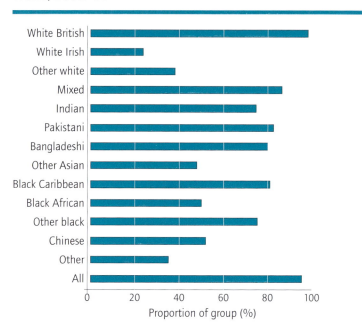

Source: *Social Trends*, 2005

Table 3: **Asylum applications in EU, 2003**

	Number of asylum seekers	Asylum seekers per 1,000 population
Austria	32,400	3.9
Sweden	31,400	3.5
Luxembourg	1,600	3.1
Ireland	7,900	2.0
Belgium	19,300	1.9
France	62,000	1.0
United Kingdom	60,000	1.0
Denmark	4,600	0.8
Netherlands	13,400	0.8
Greece	8,200	0.7
Finland	3,200	0.6
Germany	50,600	0.6
Italy	13,500	0.2
Spain	5,900	0.1
Portugal	100	–
All applications to EU-15	313,900	0.8

Source: *Social Trends*, 2005

1.3 UK Households

Size

In spring 2004 there were 24.1 million households in Great Britain. Between 1971 and 2003, the average household size fell from 2.9 to 2.4 people. The size of households has remained the same as it was in 2001, with most being one- or two-person households (Table 4)

Composition

In 2004, 70 per cent of people in private households lived in couple-family households. Since 1971 the proportion of people living in the 'traditional' family household of a couple with dependent children has fallen from just over 50 per cent to under 40 per cent, while the proportion of people living in couple-family households with no children has increased from just under 20 per cent to 25 per cent (Table 5).

1.4 Family and partnership patterns

- About 3–4 per cent of marriages fail in Britain each year, while cohabitation rates are rising.
- England and Wales have the highest divorce rates in Europe, with around 40 per cent of marriages currently ending in divorce.
- Rates of remarriage, following divorce or widowhood have dropped since the 1970s by 75 per cent for men and over 50 per cent for women.
- However, it is estimated that about one in eight children experience life in stepfamilies by the age of 16.
- 50 per cent of the 6 million carers in the UK are aged 45–64. Nearly 60 per cent are women.
- Male carers tend to be looking after spouses and women after children or parents. Twice as many women as men look after older parents

(Schuller, 2005, compiled from *Social Trends* 2004 and other sources.)

Table 4: **Size of households, Great Britain, comparisons between 1971 and 2004**

	1971	1981	1991	2001	2004
	(%)				
One person	18	22	27	29	29
Two people	32	32	34	35	35
Three people	19	17	16	16	16
Four people	17	18	16	14	14
Five people	8	7	5	5	5
Six or more people	6	4	2	2	2
All households (millions)	18.6	20.2	22.4	23.8	24.1
Average household size (number of people)	2.9	2.7	2.5	2.4	2.4

Source: *Social Trends*, 2005

Table 5: **People in households, by type of household and family, Great Britain, 1971–2004**

	1971	1981	1991	2001	2004
	(%)				
One person	6	8	11	12	13
One-family households					
Couple					
No children	19	20	23	25	25
Dependent children[a]	52	47	41	39	37
Non-dependent children only	10	10	11	8	8
Lone parent	4	6	10	12	13
Other households	9	9	4	4	4
All people in private households (millions)	53.4	53.9	55.4	56.4	56.8
People not in private households (millions)	0.9	0.8	0.8	–	–
Total population (millions)[b]	54.4	54.8	56.2	57.4	58.1

a May also include non-dependent children
b Data for 1971 to 1991 are census enumerated. Data for 2001 are 2001 mid-year estimates. Data for 2004 are 2003-based projections.

Source: *Social Trends*, 2005

1.5 Wealth and income

Wealth

In 2002 half the adult population in the UK owned only 6 per cent of total wealth (Table 6).

Gross domestic product (GDP) measures the level of income generated by economic activity in the United Kingdom in accordance with international conventions. Since 1971 the trend in GDP per head has generally been one of steady growth. However, within this long-term trend the United Kingdom is subject to cycles of weaker and stronger growth, usually referred to as the economic or business cycle (*Social Trends*, 2005). UK GDP level is about sixth among current EU members (Table 7).

Table 6: **Distribution of wealth,[a] United Kingdom, 1991–2002**

	1991	1996	2000	2001	2002
			(%)		
Marketable wealth					
Percentage of wealth owned by:[b]					
Most wealthy 1%	17	20	23	22	23
Most wealthy 5%	35	40	44	42	43
Most wealthy 10%	47	52	56	54	56
Most wealthy 25%	71	74	75	72	74
Most wealthy 50%	92	93	95	94	94
Total marketable wealth (£ billion)	1,711	2,092	3,131	3,477	3,464
Marketable wealth less value of dwellings					
Percentage of wealth owned by:[b]					
Most wealthy 1%	29	26	33	34	35
Most wealthy 5%	51	49	59	58	62
Most wealthy 10%	64	63	73	72	75
Most wealthy 25%	80	81	89	88	88
Most wealthy 50%	93	94	98	98	98

a Distribution of personal wealth. Estimates for individual years should be treated with caution as they are affected by sampling error and the particular pattern of deaths in that year.
b Adults aged 18 and over

Source: *Social Trends*, 2005

Table 7: **Gross domestic product per head, EU, 1991–2002**

	1991	1996	2002
	(€ per head)		
Luxembourg	25,200	28,400	45,000
Ireland	12,200	16,600	28,400
Austria	18,500	20,700	26,000
Denmark	17,300	20,100	25,900
Netherlands	16,900	19,300	25,800
United Kingdom	15,000	17,900	25,000
Belgium	17,000	19,000	24,700
Sweden	17,200	18,800	24,300
Finland	15,700	16,900	24,000
France	16,700	18,300	23,900
Italy	16,500	18,400	23,100
Germany	17,200	18,900	23,000
Spain	12,500	14,100	20,000
Cyprus	–	13,500	17,600
Greece	10,800	11,500	16,500
Portugal	10,500	11,700	16,200
Slovenia	9,430	11,200	15,900
Malta	–	–	15,700
Czech Republic	–	11,500	14,300
Hungary	7,310	7,900	12,400
Slovakia	–	7,400	10,900
Estonia	–	5,700	9,700
Poland	–	6,800	9,700
Lithuania	7,460	5,700	9,000
Latvia	9,500	4,900	8,200

Note: Gross domestic product at current market prices using current purchasing power standard and compiled on the basis of the European System of Accounts 1995.

Source: Eurostat

Figure 2: **Low income, by location, Great Britain, 1994–97 and 2001–04**

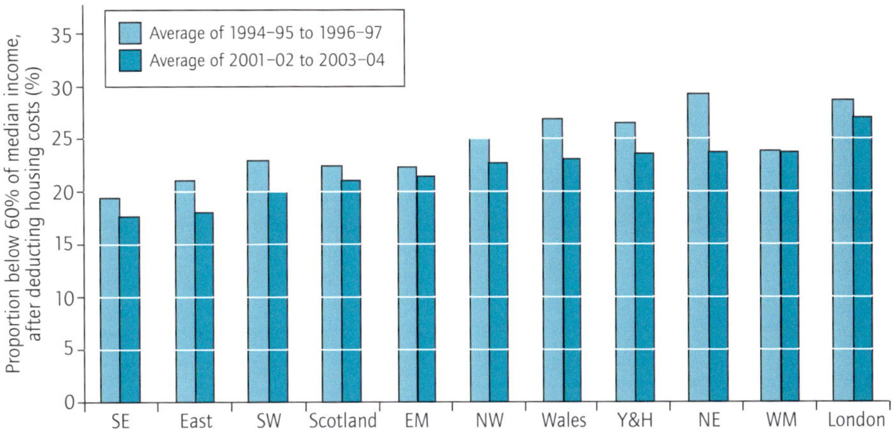

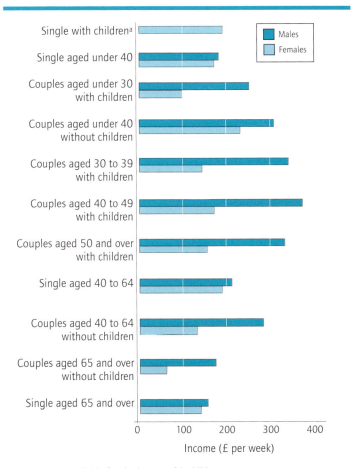

Source: Poverty.org.uk, Income graphs

Incomes

Incomes in the UK have risen steadily over the last few years, particularly for some groups and in some areas. Figure 2 shows that the proportion of people on low incomes has fallen in all regions apart from the West Midlands. London has a higher proportion than any other region

Between 2002 and 2003:

- UK real household disposable income per head rose by 1.8 per cent, compared with growth in GDP per head of 2.0 per cent.
- The 30 per cent of individuals at the top of the income distribution in Great Britain received over half of total disposable income.
- The pre-tax income of pensioners in Great Britain rose by 26 per cent in real terms between 1994–95 and 2002–03, compared with an increase of 13 per cent in real average earnings.

There are, however, real differences between the income of men and women as shown in Figure 3.

Figure 3 shows clearly the extent to which men's incomes exceed those of women throughout the life cycle. In 2002–03 in Great Britain, the median net income of women was only 60 per cent of that of men. The gap was narrowest for single people and generally widened with age. The net income of women aged under 40 was 92 per cent of that of

Figure 3: **Median net individual income, by life stage and sex, Great Britain, 2002–03**

a No estimate available for single men with children

Source: *Social Trends*, 2005

men, but only 88 per cent for those aged 40 and over.

The largest proportional income gap between men and women was among couples aged 65 and over without children. This results from wives' traditionally lower entitlements for both state and occupational pensions while their husbands are alive.

The second-largest gap was for couple-families aged under 30 with children: in such families the median net income of women was about 38 per cent of that of men. This is explained by the tendency for women to work part-time or to leave the labour force while bringing up young children. The gap then gradually closes for older couples with children, as women return to the labour market.

Low incomes

(The definition of low income used in the UK government's current targets for reducing child poverty is 60 per cent of median income, with income levels adjusted for household size and composition).

Although there has been a drop in the number of low-income families (Figure 4), in 2002–03, 17 per cent of the population were living in households with income less than 60 per cent of contemporary median disposable income (Babb *et al*, 2004).

One in six of the poorest households still do not have any type of bank/building society account – three times the rate for households on average incomes.

The overall distribution of income has changed little over the last decade: the poorest tenth have 2 per cent of total income in Great Britain.

Although work is considered to be the route out of poverty, two-fifths of people in low-income, working-age households have someone in paid work but earning very low wages. A quarter of all those earning less than £6.50 per hour are directly employed by the public sector.

Figure 4: **Numbers on low incomes, Great Britain, 1997–2004**

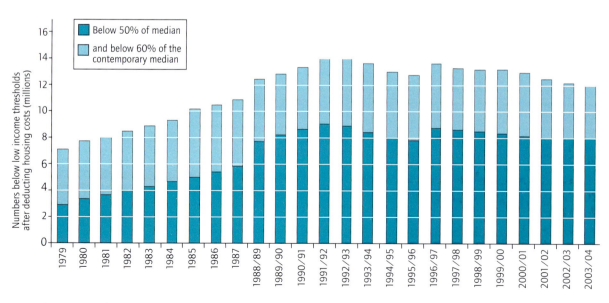

Source: Poverty.org.uk, Income graphs

By 2003–04, people receiving the state retirement pension were no more likely than non-pensioners to live in low-income households. However, around 1.2 million pensioners have no income other than their state pension and benefits – a fifth of all single pensioners and a tenth of couples (www.poverty.org.uk). Moreover, a large number of older people entitled to Council Tax Benefit and the Minimum Income Guarantee are not claiming them (Figure 5).

1.6 Pensions

- The UK state pension is about 37 per cent (including SERPS) of average earnings, compared to 70 per cent in continental Europe and 45 per cent in the US.
- 69 per cent of women receive less than the full State Pension compared to 15 per cent of men.
- Only 18 per cent of people of working age contribute either directly or via a partner to a pension scheme. Those most under-represented are women, the self-employed, those working in firms with less than 50 employees, workers in the retail, construction and leisure industries, and those earning less than £9,500.
- Direct benefit final salary schemes declined from 35 per cent to 20 per cent of employees between 1983 and 2003. Eighty-five per cent of those in the public sector participate in final salary schemes. It is estimated that only 1.6–1.8 million people in the private sector will have final salary pensions in 2020. (TAEN, 2005b).

1.7 Debt

The Griffiths Commission on Personal Debt (2005) concluded that there is a serious debt problem for roughly 3 million people. Although this is spread throughout the population, it disproportionately affects low-income families, lone parents and people in their 20s and early 30s. Up to 12 million more people struggle to repay their credit commitments from time to time.

Figure 5: **Older people receiving welfare benefits, Great Britain, 1997–2003**

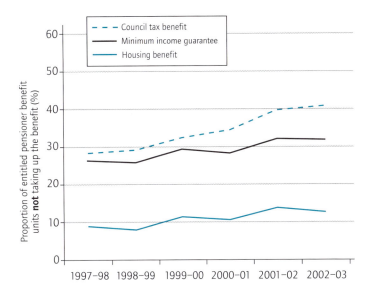

Source: Poverty.org.uk, Older People graphs

The average amount owed by debtors in October 2003 was £3,500, but there were wide variations in the amounts owed. Most debtors owed relatively small amounts (£1,000–£3,000). However, 13 per cent owed £10,000 or more. The survey found that 10 per cent of individuals considered their unsecured debt to be a heavy burden.

The Commission refers to student loans as 'a growing problem' that is likely to worsen as a result of rising tuition fees and living expenses.

1.8 Social mobility

It is becoming more difficult for people in the UK to get out of poverty. Research has found that social mobility in Britain is lower than in Canada, Germany, Sweden, Norway, Denmark and Finland. In the US levels are comparable to Britain, but there the gap between rich and poor is static, while in Britain it is getting wider.

The study found that Britain's low and declining mobility is in part due to the strong relationship between family income and educational attainment, and the fact that additional opportunities to stay in education at age 16 and age 18 are disproportionately benefiting those from better-off backgrounds. Educational participation in the 1990s was characterised by a narrowing in the achievement gap between rich and poor children at 16+ but a widening in terms of access to higher education.

When comparing those born in the 1950s and the 1970s, university graduation rates from the poorest fifth of families have increased from 6 per cent to 9 per cent, but have risen from 20 per cent to 47 per cent for the richest fifth. (Blanden *et al*, 2005).

1.9 Measures to help those on low income or out of work

One of the government's Public Service Agreement (PSA) targets is to halve the number of children in low-income households between 1998 and 2011, with an additional target to be set in the 2006 Spending Review to halve by 2010 the number of children suffering from both material deprivation and relative low income. People on low incomes or out of work can claim a range of benefits:

In-work benefits

Tax credits have been introduced to help people on low pay. In January 2004, approximately two-and-a-half million people were receiving tax credits – around double the numbers in 2000 and three times the numbers receiving the equivalent benefit (Family Credit) a decade ago. Over 90 per cent of recipients of this benefit have dependent children (New Policy Institute, 2005) (Figure 6).

Figure 6: **Working households receiving Working and Child Tax Credits, Great Britain, 1995–2004**

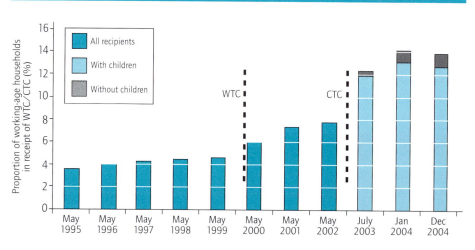

Source: Poverty.org.uk, Working age adults graphs

The income support available for working age adults without children has fallen behind support for families with children and people receiving the State Retirement Pension (Figure 7).

Out-of-work benefits

The number of working-age claimants of out-of-work benefits fell between 2003 and 20004. At November 2004:

- 13.4 per cent of people of working age were claiming a key benefit; 48 per cent of these were women
- 2.2 million people were claiming Income Support (a drop since 2003).
- 3.9 million people were receiving Housing Benefit (an increase since 2002 and 2003).
- 4.9 million people were receiving Council Tax benefit (an increase since 2002 and 2003).
- 775,000 people were claiming the Jobseeker's Allowance. Nearly three quarters of these were men.
- 2.4 million people were claiming Incapacity Benefit (a drop since 2001).
- 2.7 million were claiming Disability Living Allowance. For some years, the largest group claiming benefits for two years or more has been those who are sick or disabled.
  (DWP, 2005b) (Figure 8).

(For those in the Working Age group, key benefits are: Jobseeker's Allowance, Income Support, Incapacity Benefit, Severe Disablement Allowance and Disability Living Allowance. For Pensioners, key benefits are Minimum Income Guarantee, Incapacity Benefit, Severe Disablement Allowance, State Pension, Attendance Allowance and Disability Living Allowance.)

Figure 7: **Levels of income support for couples, United Kingdom, 1995–2004**

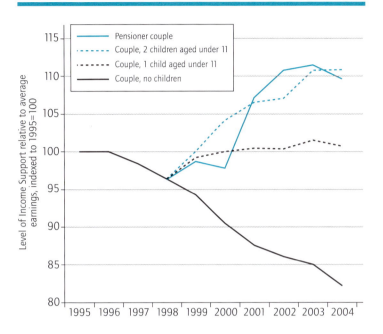

Source: Poverty.org.uk, Income graphs

Figure 8: **Groups of working-age people receiving a key benefit for two years or more, Great Britain, 1996–2004**

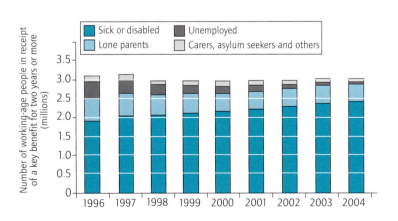

Source: Poverty.org.uk, Income graphs

1.10 Families on key benefits

In November 2004:

- 2.7 million children (21 per cent of all children in Great Britain) were living in families claiming a key benefit. (The number of children in families receiving an income-related benefit fell by 99,000 between Nov 2004 and Nov 2004, from 2.29 million to 2.19 million.)
- 58 per cent of key benefit children were in families claiming Income Support only.
- 65 per cent of children were living in families where the claimant was single.
- Of families on a key benefit with children, 66 per cent had been on benefit for at least two years. For the sick/disabled group, the figure was 75 per cent.
- The percentage of children living in families claiming a key benefit varied from 30 per cent in the London to 14 per cent in the South East (DWP, 2005b).

People over pension age

At November 2004:

- 99.9 per cent of people over State Pension age were claiming a key benefit; 37 per cent of these were men.
- 11.5 million were receiving the State Pension (continuing a sharp increase since 1995).
- 2.6 million of those aged 60 or over were claiming pension Credit/Minimum Income Guarantee.

1.11 Household expenditure

Table 8 indicates that compared with other major items, education was the lowest item of household expenditure in the UK in 2003.

Table 9 indicates, unsurprisingly, that total expenditure in 2002–03 was highest for households where the reference person was in the managerial and professional group. Their expenditure was nearly double the spending of households in the never-worked and long-term unemployed group. Spending on education by this

Table 8: **Volume of household expenditure, United Kingdom, 1971–2003**

	Indices (1971=100)					£ billion (current prices)
	1971	1981	1991	2001	2003	2003
Food and non-alcoholic drink	100	105	117	137	141	63.1
Alcohol and tobacco	100	99	92	88	91	27.3
Clothing and footwear	100	120	187	346	411	41.2
Housing, water and fuel	100	117	138	152	156	125.5
Household goods and services	100	117	160	262	267	39.1
Health	100	125	182	180	205	12.1
Transport	100	128	181	238	247	98.0
Communication	100	190	306	790	846	15.5
Recreation and culture	100	161	283	549	610	83.7
Education	100	160	199	253	232	9.6
Restaurants and hotels[a]	100	126	167	193	206	81.2
Miscellaneous goods and services	100	119	230	284	293	84.7
Total domestic household expenditure	100	121	166	220	232	681.1
of which goods	100	117	156	225	244	329.1
of which services	100	129	182	222	227	351.9
Less expenditure by foreign tourists, etc	100	152	187	210	211	−14.2
Household expenditure abroad	100	193	298	668	712	26.7
All household expenditure[b]	100	122	167	227	240	693.6

a Includes purchases of alcoholic drink.
b Includes expenditure by UK households in the United Kingdom and abroad.

Source: *Social Trends*, 2005

Table 9: **Household expenditure, by socio-economic classification,[a] United Kingdom, 2002–03**

| | Occupations | | | | |
	Managerial and professional	Intermediate	Routine and manual	Never worked[b] and long-term unemployed	All households[c]
			(£ per week)		
Food and non-alcoholic drink	52.60	44.90	43.40	30.90	42.70
Alcohol and tobacco	13.50	11.60	13.80	9.00	11.40
Clothing and footwear	33.60	25.30	24.10	24.50	22.30
Housing, fuel and power[d]	47.00	39.40	38.30	67.20	36.90
Household goods and services	49.50	29.70	26.80	13.90	30.20
Health	7.30	4.50	3.10	2.00	4.80
Transport	98.40	72.10	57.70	37.80	59.20
Communication	13.80	12.40	11.40	17.10	10.60
Recreation and culture	86.30	59.20	57.20	44.00	56.40
Education	13.20	5.10	2.10	14.80	5.20
Restaurants and hotels	58.90	38.10	35.50	42.90	35.40
Miscellaneous goods and services	53.30	35.40	30.10	18.20	33.10
Other expenditure items	109.70	69.80	52.70	17.70	58.30
All household expenditure	637.00	447.50	396.10	340.00	406.60
Average household size (number of people)	2.7	2.6	2.7	2.5	2.4

a Of the household reference person. Excludes retired households.
b Includes households where the reference person is a student.
c Includes retired households and others that are not classified.
d Excludes mortgage interest payments, water charges, council tax and Northern Ireland domestic rates. These are included in 'Other expenditure items'

Source: *Social Trends*, 2005

group was similar to that of never worked and long-term unemployed groups (which includes students) and was about two-and-a-half times the average for all households (£13.20 per week compared with £5.20).

The fact that two large occupational groups (intermediate, routine and manual workers) spend so little on education has clear implications for the projected raising of fee levels for courses and programmes that are not linked to government educational priorities.

Although households in the routine and manual group spent significantly less in total than those in the managerial and professional group, they spent more than any other group on alcohol and tobacco (*Social Trends*, 2005).

Prices

Figure 9 shows that education underwent the highest increase in price in 2003, followed by health, transport, restaurant and hotels.

The greatest fall in prices was for clothing and footwear, recreation and culture, and furniture and household goods. Of these, the largest decrease was for clothing and footwear (3.8 per cent).

Price levels vary across the UK. In 2004, London prices were nearly 10 per cent higher than the national average, while prices in Wales were nearly 7 per cent below average. The regional difference was greatest for housing costs. They ranged from nearly 29 per cent above the UK average in London to just over 32 per cent below average in Northern Ireland. Price levels were higher in London than in Wales for all goods and services, except fares and other travel costs – these were 1.0 per cent below the UK average in London and 9.5 per cent above it in Wales. Despite Northern Ireland having slightly below average overall prices, the cost of fuel and light was nearly 13 per cent above the UK average.

Figure 9: **Percentage change of consumer price index, United Kingdom, 2003**

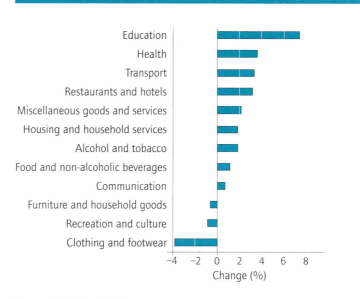

Source: *Social Trends*, 2005

1.12 Housing and homelessness

- Between 1971 and 2003 the number of dwellings in Great Britain increased by one-third, to 25 million.
- The number of owner-occupied dwellings in Great Britain increased by 44 per cent between 1981 and 2003, while the number of rented dwellings fell by 17 per cent.
- In 2003–04, 50 per cent of lone parents with dependent children in the United Kingdom rented their home from the social sector, compared with only 15 per cent of couples with dependent children.
- The average private-sector rent (after housing benefit) in England doubled between 1993–94 and 2003–04, while the average local authority rent increased by 47 per cent.

Homelessness

- The number of homeless households in England living in temporary accommodation more than doubled between March 1997 and March 2004.
- 200,000 households were accepted as 'homeless' by local authorities in England in 2003 – 25 per cent higher than in 2000. Most of these were households without dependent children.
- Female lone parents with dependent children are the group most affected by homelessness (Table 10).

However the number of homeless households without dependent children has also risen by 30 per cent, to 130,000 in 2004 (Poverty.com)

The number of homeless families in temporary accommodation has increased by 123 per cent since 1997 to nearly 100,000 by the end of 2003–04 (*Working Brief*, 2005a).

Table 10: **Homelessness,[a] by household composition, England, 2002–03**

	(%)
One person	
Males	18
Females	19
Lone parent with dependent children	
Males	3
Females	35
Couple with dependent children	15
Other households	10
All households	100

a Households accepted as homeless and in priority need by local authorities.

Source: *Social Trends*, 2005

1.13 Health

Although overall life expectancy has increased over the last two decades, and the numbers of premature deaths among working-age adults has dropped since 1992, inequality in life expectancy has widened, mainly among women. The gap is now 4.5 years between the highest and lowest social classes (TAEN, 2005b). In addition:

- Premature deaths are much higher in Scotland than in England or Wales.
- The proportion of adults in England who were obese increased between 1993 and 2003: from 13 to 23 per cent of men and from 16 to 23 per cent of women.
- In 2003–04, 40 per cent of men and 23 per cent of women exceeded the recommended daily benchmarks for sensible drinking on at least one day in the previous week.
- In 2003–04, smoking was most common among adults in routine and manual households (35 per cent of men and 31 per cent of women) and least prevalent among those in managerial

and professional households (20 per cent and 17 per cent respectively).
- The incidence of lung cancer in males has fallen by more than 40 per cent over the past 20 years, mainly as a result of the earlier decline in smoking.
- The suicide rate for men aged 25 to 44 in the United Kingdom doubled between 1971 and 1998 to 27 per 100,000; in 2003 it had dropped to 23 per 100,000.
- In 2002–03 two-thirds of 60 to 74 year old men in England, and three-fifths of women of the same age, who reported that they had difficulties with daily activities or mobility.
- Almost half of all adults in the poorest fifth of the population aged 45–64 have a limiting long-standing illness or disability, twice the rate for those on average incomes.
- Women on below-average incomes are twice as likely to be obese as women on above-average incomes.
- Adults in the poorest fifth are twice as likely to be at risk of developing a mental illness as those

Figure 10: **Infant mortality rates, by social class background, Great Britain, 1993–2002**

Source: Poverty.org.uk, Health graphs

on average incomes. Women are more likely to develop a mental illness than men (*Social Trends*, 2005; New Policy Institute, 2005; Poverty.com).

Figure 10 shows that infant mortality is directly related to social class:

1.14 Drug use

According to the British Crime Survey (BCS) 2003–4:

- More than a million people in England and Wales use Class A drugs, half a million of them doing so regularly.
- Cannabis remains the most popular drug among all age groups. The drug was reclassified in January 2004 from Class B to Class C)
- Cocaine is the second most popular drug after cannabis, with more than three-quarters of a million people saying they have used it in the last year.

- 2.4 per cent of people aged 16–59 had taken cocaine in the last year, compared with 2.1 per cent in the 2002–03 survey and 0.6 per cent in 1996.
- Usage of the drug was most common among 25–34 year olds. In 1996 only 1.1 per cent of this age group had taken cocaine in the previous 12 months, but by 2003–04 that figure had increased to 4.5 per cent.
- Use of Ecstasy remained constant at 2 per cent of those surveyed taking it at least once a year.
- Magic mushrooms consumption increased by around 40 per cent (although from July 2005, the 2005 Drugs Act stopped them being sold openly).
- Heroin and crack cocaine are the least-used Class A drugs, with just 0.1 per cent and 0.2 per cent of those surveyed taking them.

Table 11: **Participation in community and voluntary activities, by highest qualification level, England and Wales, 2003**

Highest qualification level[a]	Civic participation	Informal volunteering	Formal volunteering	Respondents
	(%)			(Number)
Degree or equivalent	49	73	60	1,635
Higher education below degree	42	71	49	1,123
GCE A-Level or equivalent	40	69	48	1,034
GCSE Grades A–C or equivalent	38	66	46	1,435
GCSE Grades D–E or equivalent	35	65	38	417
Foreign or other qualifications	38	56	31	352
No qualifications	29	49	24	1,831
All[a]	38	62	42	9,483

a The qualification figures exclude respondents aged 70 or over. These are included in the figures for all respondents

Source: Home Office, 2003

1.15 Social and civic participation

The Home Office Citizenship Survey (2003) shows that there is a strong correlation between qualification level and community and civic participation. Those with the lowest qualifications are the least likely to engage in community or civic activity (Table 11).

Other groups unlikely to participate in social and civic activities are:

- Those working in lower-paid occupations.
- The unemployed.
- Lone parents.
- Some minority ethnic groups, particularly Bangladeshi and Pakistani.

Young people and elderly people are less likely than those in their middle years to join in the activities of social organisations or participate in civic life. However, young people have more active friendship and relative networks than other age groups.

Lack of resources such as time and money is the most frequently cited barrier to participation in social and civic activities. Other barriers include poor health or a disability and not having own transport. Lack of information regarding opportunities and lack of awareness of the need for help also prevents people from engaging in social and civic activities. Those who think that their contribution will have an impact are more likely to participate than those who think they will not make any difference (*Social Trends*, 2005).

The Home Office Citizenship Survey in 2001 found that in England and Wales, the main incentives identified for getting involved in formal volunteering, were being asked directly to (44 per cent) and shared activity with friends or family (40 per cent). In addition, 25 per cent of people said that improving skills or getting qualifications was an incentive.

Volunteering

Table 12 shows the main kinds of contribution made by volunteers.

Civic participation

There has been a general growth in civic participation since 1986 and especially since 2000. Table 13 shows the most common kinds of activity.

Thirty-nine per cent of the UK electorate voted in the 2004 European Parliament elections, an increase of 15 percentage points on the previous election in 1999.

Non-participation

Nine million adults who are not in paid work or full-time education do not participate in any social, political or community organisations (Poverty.org).

Table 12: **Type of help given by formal volunteers,[a] England and Wales, 2001 and 2003**

	2001	2003
	(%)	
Organising or helping to run an activity or event	61	57
Raising or handling money	56	54
Leading a group/being a member of a committee	44	40
Giving other practical help	40	32
Provide transport/driving	31	29
Giving advice/information/counselling	34	28
Secretarial, administrative or clerical work	24	24
Befriending/mentoring people	–	19
Representing	20	16
Campaigning	14	9
Any other help	8	9

a Adults aged 16 and over who volunteered formally at least once a month in the last 12 months before interview.

Source: *Social Trends*, 2005

Table 13: **Participation in civic activities, England, 1986–2002[a]**

	1986	1989	1991	1994	2000	2002	Change 1986 to 2002
				(%)			
Signed a petition	34	41	53	39	42	43	+9
Contacted their MP	11	15	17	14	16	17	+6
Contacted radio, TV or newspaper	3	4	4	5	6	7	+4
Gone on a protest or demonstration	6	8	9	9	10	12	+6
Spoken to an influential person	3	3	5	3	4	6	+3
Contacted a government department[b]	3	3	4	3	4	–	–
Formed a group of like-minded people	2	3	2	3	2	2	0
Raised the issue in an organisation they already belong to	5	4	5	4	5	6	+1
None of these	56	48	37	53	47	46	–10

a Figures do not add to 100 per cent as more than one response could be given.
b Question not asked in 2002.

Source: Babb *et al*, 2004

1.16 Lifestyle and leisure

Social Trends, 2004 and 2005 indicate that:

- Watching television is still the main leisure activity reported by people in all age groups (*Social Trends*, 2005).
- There were 171 million cinema admissions in 2004, the second-highest number for over 30 years.
- UK residents took 41.2 million holidays abroad in 2003, six times the number in 1971.
- In 2002–03, 59 per cent of adults in Great Britain had participated in a sport, game or physical activity in the four weeks before interview, 6 percentage points lower than in 1990–91. As is to be expected, participation in sport or physical activity declines with age (Table 14).

1.17 Ownership of and access to new technology

In 2002–03:

- 70 per cent of household had mobile phones.
- 55 per cent of households had a home computer.
- 83 per cent had a CD player.
- 31 per cent of households owned a DVD player.
- 45 per cent of households (10.9 million) could access the Internet from home.
  (*Social Trends*, 2005)

Internet access

Household Internet access varies across the UK. The highest levels of access in 2002–03 were in London, the South East and the East of England, where around 50 per cent of households could connect to the Internet at home. In contrast, only around 35 per cent of households in Northern Ireland and Wales could do so. This reflects regional differences in computer ownership. In 2002–03, around 45 per cent of households in Northern Ireland and Wales had a computer, compared with around 60 per cent in London, the South East and the East of England (*Social Trends*, 2005) (Figure 11).

Table 14: **Adult participation in sport or physical activity,[a] by age, Great Britain, 1987–2003**

	1987	1990–91	1996–97	2002–03
		(%)		
16–19	86	87	86	77
20–24	77	81	81	69
25–29	74	78	77	70
30–44	71	73	73	67
45–59	56	63	63	59
60–69	47	54	55	50
70 and over	26	31	31	30
All aged 16 and over	61	65	64	59

a Includes walking two miles or more for recreational purposes.

Source: *Social Trends*, 2005

Figure 11: **Households with home access to the Internet, by region, United Kingdom, 2002–03**

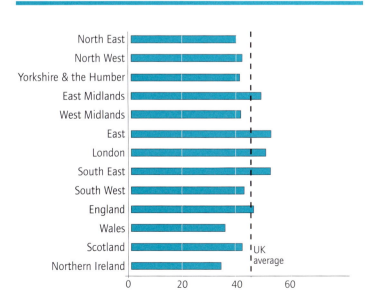

Source: *Social Trends*, 2005

Patterns of access and use

- 58 per cent of adults in Great Britain had used the Internet in the three months prior to interview in 2003–04 – a rise of 10 percentage points since 2001–02 (ONS, 2004).

- Levels of Internet access are linked to household income. In 2002–03 only 12 per cent of households in the United Kingdom with gross household income below £123 a week (the lowest income decile group) had access to the Internet. In contrast, 85 per cent of households with gross income of over £1,085 (the highest income decile group) had access.

- Households with children are more likely than those without children to own a computer or have Internet access. In 2004, 87 per cent of children aged 9 to 15 lived in a household with a computer. Of these, 62 per cent lived in a household with one computer, and 38 per cent lived in a household with more than one computer. Twenty-three per cent of children had broadband access at home.

- Use of the Internet in the United Kingdom is far higher among children than among adults. According to the UK *Children Go Online* study, which surveyed 9 to 15 year olds between January and March 2004, 74 per cent of children had accessed the Internet via a computer from home and 93 per cent had accessed it at school. Information gathering and schoolwork were their main reasons for use (Citizens Online, 2005).

- There has been growth in Internet use among those aged 55 and over. Between 2001–02 and 2003–04, the proportion of people in this age group who had used the Internet in the three months prior to interview rose from 18 per cent to 27 per cent. This compares with an increase from 63 per cent to 73 per cent among people aged under 55.

- Among people aged 55 and over who used the Internet in 2003–04, a considerable proportion used it every day or almost every day (38 per cent), while 10 per cent used it less than once a month.

- Overall, 37 per cent of all adults, and 69 per cent of those aged 55 and over, had never used

Table 15: **Purpose of Internet use, by age,[a] Great Britain, 2002–03**

	16–34	35–54	55 and over	All adults
	(%)			
Using email	83	84	85	84
Searching for information about goods or services	80	84	74	80
Searching for information about travel and accommodation	63	74	70	69
General browsing or surfing	76	66	49	67
Buying goods, tickets or services	51	52	42	50
Internet banking	34	39	33	36
Activities related specifically to employment	39	37	17	35
Reading or downloading online news	37	34	25	34
Activities related to an education course	38	23	11	28
Playing or downloading music	37	18	12	25
Other educational activities	26	26	18	25
Downloading other software	27	22	18	23
Listening to web radios	20	13	9	15
Other financial services	7	9	9	8

a Adults who used the Internet in the previous three months.

Source: *Social Trends*, 2005

the Internet in 2003–04. The majority of people in the 55 and over age group who had not used the Internet said that they did not want or need it, or had no interest in it (57 per cent).

- The most popular activities across all age groups who had used the Internet in the three months prior to interview in 2003– 04 were use of email (84 per cent) and searching for information about goods and services (80 per cent). People aged 55 and over were less likely than 16 to 34 year olds to have 'surfed' the Internet, downloaded music or software, read or downloaded online news or purchased over the Internet (Table 15) (*Social Trends*, 2005).

Unsurprisingly, the use of the Internet for educational purposes is highest among younger adults and for those on higher incomes. This reflects levels of post-16 participation in education and training, as seen in Section 4.

1.18 Crime and custody

Drug offences and violence against the person were the most common recorded crimes.
The rate of recorded and detected crimes was significantly higher in Scotland than in other parts of the UK.

Table 16 shows the rates of indictable offences which individuals were found guilty of or cautioned for in 2003, by sex and age.

Table 16: **Rates of indictable offences which individuals were found guilty of or cautioned, by sex and age, England and Wales, 2003**

	10–15	16–24	25–34	35 and over	All aged 10 and over
	(Rates per 10,000 population)				(Thousands)
Males					
Theft and handling stolen goods	81	162	96	18	124.3
Drug offences	18	156	62	10	86.2
Violence against the person	34	78	34	10	55.7
Burglary	26	45	21	2	29.3
Criminal damage	14	19	7	2	13.2
Robbery	7	13	4	–	6.8
Sexual offences	3	4	3	2	5.6
Other indictable offences[a]	10	101	62	13	72.1
All indictable offences	193	577	288	56	393.2
Females					
Theft and handling stolen goods	52	62	32	6	49.3
Drug offences	3	15	9	2	10.6
Violence against the person	13	13	6	2	11.1
Burglary	3	3	1	–	2.0
Criminal damage	3	2	1	–	1.8
Robbery	2	1	–	–	0.9
Sexual offences	–	–	–	–	0.1
Other indictable offences[a]	3	19	14	3	15.4
All indictable offences	78	116	64	12	91.2

a Other indictable offences includes fraud and forgery and indictable motoring.

Source: *Social Trends*, 2005

Prison population

In April 2005 the number of people in prison was 76,035, compared to 75,544 in April 2004 (*Working Brief*, 2005b), and is apparently still growing.

Table 17 shows that the profile of the prison population in England and Wales has changed little in the past few years, with the proportions of white male and black male inmates increasing and decreasing by 1 per cent respectively between 2002 and 2003. The total female prison population has decreased slightly, though grown by two percentage points among black women.

Table 17: **British nationals in prison, by ethnic group, England and Wales, 2001–03**

	2001	2002	2003
		(%)	
Males			
White	85	84	83
Black	11	11	12
Asian	2	3	3
Chinese and other	2	2	3
		(Thousands)	
Total male population	55.7	59.1	59.0
		(%)	
Females			
White	86	84	83
Black	12	11	13
Asian	1	1	1
Chinese and other	2	3	3
		(Thousands)	
Total female population	3.0	3.5	3.4

Source: *Social Trends*, 2005

Section 2
The labour market:
occupational change, employment patterns and skill needs

2.1 Labour market and occupational trends

A number of factors are producing changes in occupational and employment patterns:

- Changes and advances in technology resulting in automation substituting for some jobs.
- Transference of some jobs (manufacturing, data processing, call centres) to locations abroad with lower labour costs.
- Outsourcing of certain functions (cleaning, security) within the production sector to the service sector.
- Increases in real incomes, resulting in higher expenditure on items such as leisure, entertainment and health care.

As a consequence of these factors, there have been increases in employment in business services, distribution and transport, and non-market services such as health and education.

Sector changes

Although the total number of jobs has risen since 1997, the number of jobs in manufacturing, construction and other construction industries has been falling (Figure 12). By 2004, the number of male employee jobs in manufacturing had fallen to 18 per cent (compared with 28 per cent in 1984). By contrast, jobs in the public and voluntary sectors have been increasing.

The largest increase in jobs over the last 20 years has been in financial and business services, which accounted for about one in five of both male and female employee jobs in June 2004 (Table 18).

Alongside these trends there has been an increase in the share and number of people employed in higher-level managerial, professional and service

Figure 12: **Occupational trends, United Kingdom, 1997–2004**

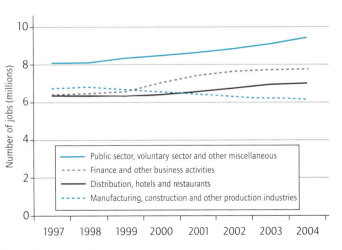

Source: Poverty.org.uk

Table 18: **Proportion of jobs, by sex and industry, United Kingdom, 1984–2004**

	Males			Females		
	1984	1994	2004	1984	1994	2004
	(%)			(%)		
Distribution, hotels, catering and repairs	18	20	23	26	26	26
Financial and business services	12	17	21	14	17	19
Manufacturing	28	24	18	16	11	7
Public administration, education and health	14	14	14	34	36	38
Transport and communication	10	10	8	2	2	3
Construction	8	7	8	2	2	1
Agriculture	2	2	1	1	1	1
Energy and water supply	4	2	1	1	–	–
Other community, social and personal services	3	4	5	5	5	6
All employee jobs (=100%) (millions)	12.3	11.3	13.3	10.2	11.7	12.9

Source: *Social Trends*, 2005

occupations and a decline in the share and number employed in lower-level manual and non-manual occupations.

Differences in workers' occupational patterns

Occupational patterns among those of working age differ by qualification, sex and ethnic group.

Qualification level

Workers with low skills and qualifications are disproportionately employed in wholesale, retailing and motor trades; manufacturing; health and social work, and transport, storage and communication

Sex

The occupational patterns of men and women remain sharply differentiated. In spring 2004, just over one-fifth of women in employment were employed in administrative and secretarial work, while men were most likely to be employed in skilled trade occupations or as managers and senior officials. These occupations were among the ones least likely to be followed by women. Women were considerably more likely than men to be employed in personal services and in sales and customer services.

Table 19: **Employment, by sex and occupation, United Kingdom, 2004**

	Males	Females
	(%)	
Managers and senior officials	18	10
Professional	13	11
Associate professional and technical	13	14
Administrative and secretarial	5	22
Skilled trades	19	2
Personal service	2	14
Sales and customer service	5	12
Process, plant and machine operatives	12	2
Elementary	12	12
All occupations	100	100

Source: *Social Trends*, 2005

Only professional, associate professional and technical occupations and elementary occupations are almost equally likely to be followed by both men and women (Table 19). (NB the table is based on jobs rather than people – one person may have more than one job).

Ethnic group

In 2002–03:

- Between 16 and 18 per cent of people from Indian, Chinese, white Irish, other non-British white and other ethnic groups were employed in professional occupations, either as employees or self-employed, compared with 11 per cent of white British people. The proportion of Indian men working as doctors, at 5 per cent, was almost ten times the rate for white British men.

- The lowest rates of professionals, managers and senior officials were found in the black groups, Bangladeshis and Pakistanis (less than 10 per cent each). There was a similar pattern across the ethnic groups.

- One in six Pakistani men in employment were taxi drivers or chauffeurs, compared with 1 in 100 white British men. One in three Bangladeshi men were either cooks or waiters, compared with 1 in 100 white British men.

- Among women in employment, around 1 in 10 black African women and 1 in 12 white Irish women were nurses, compared with only 1 in 32 white British women.

- Indian women were seven times more likely than white British women to be working as sewing machinists, and four times more likely to be working as packers, bottlers, canners and fillers.

- Low-skilled migrants are over-represented in the agricultural, hotel and restaurant and private household sectors (OECD, 2004b).

2. 2 Employment and economic activity rates

The United Kingdom is currently experiencing high rates of employment. In August 2005 there were 28.76 million people in employment, the highest figure since comparable records began in 1971 and over 2 million more than in 1989.

Table 20 shows overall rates of employment and economic activity (which includes those not in employment but seeking work).

Table 20: **Economic activity, United Kingdom, 1989 and 2004**

	1989			2004		
	Males	Females	All	Males	Females	All
	(Millions)			(Millions)		
Economically active						
In employment						
Full-time employees	11.6	6.0	17.5	11.4	6.8	18.1
Part-time employees	0.5	4.5	5.0	1.2	5.2	6.4
Self-employed	2.7	0.8	3.5	2.7	1.0	3.6
Others in employment[a]	0.3	0.2	0.5	0.1	0.1	0.2
All in employment	15.1	11.5	26.6	15.4	13.0	28.4
Unemployed	1.2	0.9	2.1	0.8	0.6	1.4
All economically active	**16.3**	**12.4**	**28.7**	**16.2**	**13.6**	**29.8**
Economically inactive	**5.2**	**10.8**	**16.0**	**6.7**	**10.8**	**17.5**

a Those on government-supported training and employment programmes and, for 2004, also unpaid family workers.

Source: *Labour Force Survey*, 2004

Regional variations

UK employment rates vary by region and area. Between March and May 2005, the overall UK employment rate was 74.7 per cent. The rates for different countries of the UK were:

England:	75.1
Scotland:	75.1
Wales:	71.2
Northern Ireland:	68.2

In 2003–04, some of the highest rates of employment were in southern and central England and Scotland, with a number of areas having employment rates over 80 per cent. The highest overall rates in the UK were in the Shetland Islands and Orkney Islands in Scotland and in Wokingham in England (over 83 per cent).

In England the areas with the highest employment rates were the East and South East, and those with the lowest, London and the North East (Table 21). However, there are variations within individual areas: in 2003–04, the London Borough of Newham had the lowest employment rate in the UK (52 per cent), while the borough of Havering had a much higher one (80 per cent); Manchester inner-city area had one of the lowest rates (60 per cent) while Stockport had a far higher one (80 per cent).

Total employment in England is expected to continue to grow over the medium term by around 1.5 million jobs, mostly part-time (LSC, 2005a).

EU comparisons

In March 2000 the European Council agreed an aim to achieve an overall European Union (EU) working-age employment rate of 70 per cent by 2010 and, for women, a rate of over 60 per cent. (The EU defines working age as people aged 15 to 64 and UK figures used in comparisons relate to people in this age group.)

Table 21: **Employment rates of working-age population, England, 2004–05**

	Working age population	Overall employment rate	
		2004–05	2003–04
	(Thousands)	(%)	(%)
England	30,360	74.8	74.6
North East	1,521	70.2	68.6
North West	4,086	72.9	72.8
Yorkshire & Humber	3,034	74.4	74.0
East Midlands	2,579	75.6	75.3
West Midlands	3,191	73.8	73.4
East of England	3,309	78.8	78.6
London	4,770	69.2	69.3
South East	4,922	78.8	79.0
South West	2,950	78.6	78.6

Source: *English Local Labour Force Survey*, 2004/2005

Table 22: **Employment rates,ᵃ by sex, EU comparison, 2003**

	Males	Females	All		Males	Females	All
	(%)				(%)		
EU–15				**Accession countries**			
Denmark	79.6	70.5	75.1	Cyprus	78.8	60.2	69.2
Netherlands	80.9	65.8	73.5	Czech Republic	73.1	56.3	64.7
Sweden	74.2	71.5	72.9	Estonia	67.2	59.0	62.9
United Kingdom	78.1	65.3	71.8	Slovenia	67.4	57.6	62.6
Austria	76.4	61.7	69.0	Latvia	66.1	57.9	61.8
Portugal	75.0	61.4	68.1	Lithuania	64.0	58.4	61.1
Finland	69.7	65.7	67.7	Slovakia	63.3	52.2	57.7
Ireland	75.0	55.8	65.4	Hungary	63.5	50.9	57.0
Germany	70.9	59.0	65.0	Malta	74.5	33.6	54.2
France	69.4	57.2	63.2	Poland	56.5	46.0	51.2
Luxembourg	73.3	52.0	62.7				
Spain	73.2	46.0	59.7	EU–15 average	72.7	56.1	64.4
Belgium	67.3	51.8	59.6				
Greece	72.4	43.8	57.8	EU–25 average	70.9	55.1	63.0
Italy	69.6	42.7	56.1				

a People aged 15 to 64.

Source: *Labour Force Survey*, Eurostat

In 2003, the overall employment rate in the European Union was 63 per cent. Together with Denmark, the Netherlands and Sweden, the UK was one of only four EU-25 countries with an employment rate above the 2010 target (Table 22).

Sex differences

The average employment rate in the EU-25 was 71 per cent for males and 55 per cent for females. The lowest employment rates for females were in the southern European countries of Greece, Italy and Malta. The north European countries of Sweden, Denmark, the Netherlands and Finland had the highest rates. Among males, the rates in 2003 ranged from 57 per cent in Poland to 81 per cent in the Netherlands.

The UK had the fourth-highest male rate and fifth-highest female employment rates in the EU.

In spring 2004, the UK male working-age employment rate was 79 per cent, roughly the same proportion as in spring 1984. However, women's employment rates grew gradually over the period from 59 per cent to 70 per cent. (*Social Trends*, 2005). The reasons for this are partly attributed to the greater willingness of women to take lower quality and lower pay jobs and a greater adaptability to career change (Grattan, 2005).

Women with young children are around half as likely as men with young children to be in employment, although they are now increasingly likely to return to work within a year of having a baby. In 2002, 72 per cent of women returned to work after a birth, compared to only 24 per cent in 1979 (DTI, 2004).

Between 1994 and 2003, the employment rate for lone parents rose from 42 per cent to 53 per cent. Lone mothers with a pre-school child aged under five are less likely to be working (33 per cent in spring 2004) than those who have a partner (58 per cent). This differential decreases as the child gets older.

Age differences

Between 1994 and 2003 the employment rate for people aged over 50 increased from 64 per cent to 70 per cent. There are now about 1.3 million more people over 50 and 0.6 million more people aged 18 to 49 in the workforce than in 1997 (Table 23).

However, the improvement has been concentrated in a limited number of business sectors, such as retail and financial services. It is not yet widely spread through the economy and a high proportion of the over-50 group work part-time. Since the employment figures include anyone working more than one hour per week, the figures showing an increase in employment among older adults should be viewed with caution.

Given the demographic changes outlined in Section 1, increased and longer engagement by older people in the labour market will be a crucial issue in coming years.

In 2004, 65 per cent of men aged between 33 and 64 and 68 per cent of women aged 50–59 were employed. The Department of Work and Pensions report, *Opportunity Age: Meeting the challenges of ageing in the 21st century* (DWP, 2005a), sets out strategies to achieve an employment rate of 80 per cent. Targets include to get one million people off Incapacity Benefit and to bring 0.3 million more single parents and one million people over 50 into employment.

Figure 13: **Employment rates, by sex, United Kingdom, 1971–2004**

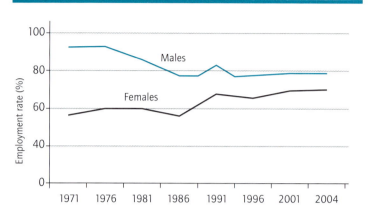

Source: *Social Trends*, 2005

Table 23: **Employment change, by age, United Kingdom, 1997–2004**

	18–24	25–49	50–SPA[a]	Post-SPA
Employment (millions)				
1997	3.3	16.6	5.2	0.8
2004	3.5	17.0	6.3	1.0
Change 1997–2004	+0.2	+0.4	+1.1	+0.2
Employment rate (%)				
1997	66	79	64	8
2004	67	81	70	9
% Change 1997–2004	+1	+2	+6	+1

a SPA=state pension age

Source: Grattan, 2005

Qualification differences

In the UK, employment rates increase generally with the level of qualification. In 2004 those with no qualifications were far less likely to be employed (49 per cent) than those with a degree (88 per cent); in spring 2004, 90 per cent of men and 86 per cent of women who had a degree or the equivalent were in employment. This compares with 55 per cent of men and 44 per cent of women who did not have any qualifications (Table 24).

Ninety-one per cent of employees in professional occupations held two or more A-levels, or a higher-level qualification, compared with 65 per cent of managers and senior officials, 22 per cent of process, plant and machine operatives and 21 per cent of those in elementary occupations. The difference in employment rates between men and women generally decreases as the level of qualification increases. For those with a degree or equivalent there was a gap of 4 percentage points in employment rates between men and women, compared with 12 percentage points for those with qualifications at NVQ level 1 and below (*Social Trends*, 2005).

The qualifications profile of the workforce in England has improved significantly since 1994 when 40 per cent of those in employment had a qualification at Level 3 or higher. By 2004, the corresponding figure was 50 per cent. This trend is attributed to the 'massive expansion' in participation in higher education and the fact that many of those acquiring intermediate-level qualifications (Level 3) go on to obtain even higher level qualifications (LSC, 2005a).

Employment patterns

About three-quarters of all jobs are full-time. In spring 2004, almost half of male, and nearly a quarter of female, managers and senior officials in the United Kingdom usually worked over 45 hours a week. However, flexible working patterns have been steadily increasing across the workforce for both full- and part-time workers (Table 25).

Table 24: **Employment rate,[a] by sex and highest qualification, United Kingdom, 2004**

	Males	Females	All
		(%)	
Degree or equivalent	90	86	88
Higher education	87	84	85
GCE A-Level or equivalent	80	73	77
Trade apprenticeship	83	72	81
GCSE grades A* to C or equivalent	80	72	75
Qualifications at NVQ level 1 and below	77	65	71
Other qualifications – level unknown	79	65	73
No qualifications	55	44	49
All[b]	79	70	74

a The percentage of the working age population in employment. Males aged 16 to 64, females aged 16 to 59.
b Includes those who did not state their highest qualification.

Source: *Social Trends*, 2005

Table 25: **Employees with flexible working patterns,[a] United Kingdom, 2004**

	Males	Females	All employees
		(%)	
Full-time employees			
Flexible working hours	9.2	14.6	11.3
Annualised working hours	5.0	4.8	4.9
Four-and-a-half day week	1.5	0.7	1.2
Term-time working	1.2	5.5	2.8
Nine-day fortnight	0.3	0.3	0.3
Any flexible working pattern[b]	17.4	26.2	20.7
Part-time employees			
Flexible working hours	5.3	8.1	7.6
Annualised working hours	3.1	4.3	4.0
Term-time working	4.2	11.2	9.9
Job sharing	1.0	2.7	2.4
Any flexible working pattern[b]	15.0	27.0	24.7

a Percentages are based on totals which exclude people who did not state whether or not they had a flexible working arrangement. Respondents could give more than one answer.
b Includes other categories of flexible working not separately identified.

Source: *Social Trends*, 2005

The low-skilled represent the largest share of the working-age population across employed as well as unemployed and inactive categories (OECD, 2004b).

Part-time and temporary employment

The proportion of full-time employees is high between the ages of 20 and 54 but declines among those aged 55 and over. In spring 2004, 26 per cent of employees were working part time.

Table 26 shows that part-time work is particularly prevalent at both ends of the age spectrum (Newton *et al*, 2005). Around four in five part-time employees are women (see Table 20). Women are also more likely than men to be temporary workers, and workers in temporary employment are more likely to working on a fixed period contract than in agency temping or in casual or seasonal jobs.

Self-employment

In spring 2004, 3.6 million people were self-employed in the United Kingdom, about 13 per cent of all those in employment. Most self-employed are men – 73 per cent in spring 2004. 18 per cent of over-50s in work are self-employed compared to 12 per cent under 50. After pension age this rises to 25 per cent.

Men and women vary considerably in the type of self-employed work they undertake. Almost 33 per cent of self-employed men work in the construction industry while almost 25 per cent of self-employed women work in 'other services' – community, social and personal services – and over 20 per cent in public administration, education and health. Fewer than 1 in

12 self-employed men worked in each of these industries.

There are some differences between ethnic groups. In 2004, 23 per cent of Pakistani and 18 per cent of Chinese people in employment in Great Britain were self-employed. This compares with around one in ten white British people and fewer than one in ten black people (Figure 14).

Figure 14: **Self-employment, by ethnic group, Great Britain, 2002–03**

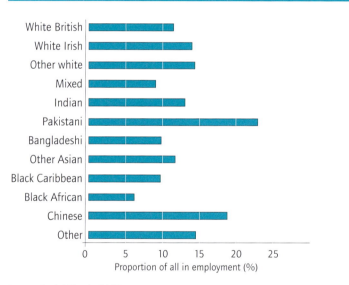

Source: *Social Trends*, 2005

Table 26: **Full- and part-time employment, by age, United Kingdom, Spring 2004**

	16–19	20–24	25–29	30–34	35–39	40–44	45–49	50–54	55–59	60–64	65–69	70 plus	Total
						(%)[a]							
Full-time	42	77	85	80	75	76	79	77	71	60	29	22	74
Part-time	58	23	15	20	25	24	21	23	29	40	71	78	26
Total (Thousands)	1,475	2,493	2,784	3,358	3,710	3,617	3,207	2,897	2,583	1,219	349	170	27,863

a Percentage of working population in age-group

Source: *Labour Force Survey*, Spring 2004

Home working

More than 2 million workers work from home, and 8 million spend some of their time working from home (ONS quoted in Campbell, 2005). This trend has been driven by the Internet and higher-speed broadband services, combined with increases in transport and other costs.

Economic activity rates

Economic activity rates differ from employment rates as they include, as well as people in work, those wanting and/or looking for work. The gap between economic activity rates for men and women was 10 percentage points in 2004 (Figure 15).

Economic activity rates in the United Kingdom also differ with age. In spring 2004, rates for men were highest for 25 to 34 and 35 to 49-year-olds: 92 per cent for both groups. For women, they were highest for 35- to 49-year-olds (78 per cent).

For people over the state pension age, economic activity rates are 9 per cent for men aged 65 and over, and 10 per cent for women aged 60 and over. Of those under state pension age, young people aged 16 to 17 had the lowest economic activity rates.

Economic inactivity after 50 is higher in Wales and Scotland than in England. In the North East 42 per cent of men aged 50 to 65+ are inactive, compared to 21 per cent in the South East.

Figure 15: **Economic activity rates, by sex, United Kingdom, 1994–2004**

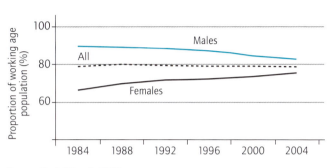

Source: *Social Trends*, 2005

Factors affecting employment and economic activity
The main factors affecting economic activity or inactivity are:

- age,
- health/disability,
- family and domestic responsibilities,
- level of qualification.

For young adults, economic activity is inevitably affected by whether or not they are in full-time education. Among those not in full-time education in spring 2004, young men (aged 16–24) were more likely than young women to be economically active – 91 per cent and 78 per cent, respectively. Of those in full-time education, young women had higher economic activity rates than young men (50 per cent and 41 per cent, respectively) (*Labour Force Survey*, 2004).

2.3 Unemployment/economic inactivity

In spring 2004, there were 7.8 million economically inactive people of working age in the United Kingdom.

The number of people who are officially (ILO) unemployed (850,000) has halved over the last decade (Figure 16). However, a further 1.5 million people are economically inactive but want paid work, slightly less than a decade ago. As a result, the total number of people wanting paid work is around three times higher than the official unemployment figures.

Long-term (2 years +) unemployed

70,000 unemployed people were claiming out-of-work benefits for two years or more in 2004 compared with 440,000 in 1994. However, the number of long-term claimants who are sick or disabled has increased by a third since 1996 and now stands at 2.4 million.

Eighty per cent of long-term claimants of out-of-work benefits are sick or disabled and a further 17 per cent are lone parents. Only 2 per cent are officially unemployed (New Policy Institute, 2005).

Unemployment rates by region

The general fall in unemployment over a decade can be seen clearly in Figure 17. The highest rates in 2004 were in London, Scotland, the West Midlands and the North East

In April 2005, the patterns were still the same: the region with the highest unemployment rate was London at 7.1 per cent, followed by Scotland at 5.6 per cent, the North East at 5.4 per cent, and Northern Ireland and the North West at 4.8 per cent (*Working Brief*, 2005).

Figure 16: **Rates of unemployment and economic inactivity, United Kingdom, 1995–2004**

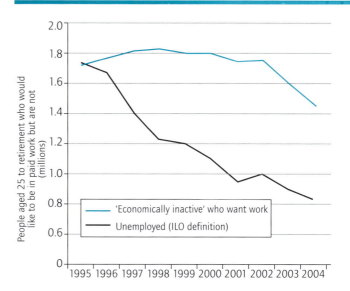

Source: Poverty.org uk

Figure 17: **Unemployment rates, by region and nation, United Kingdom, 1993–2004**

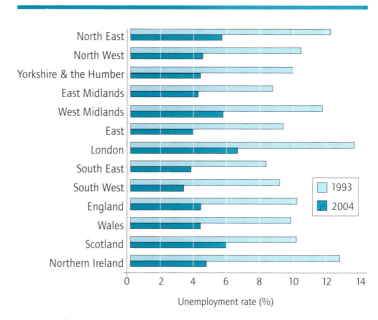

Source: *Social Trends*, 2005

Sex differences in economic inactivity and unemployment

Of the 7.8 million economically inactive people of working age in the UK 60 per cent are women, reflecting both women's full-time involvement in home management and family responsibilities and the larger number of older women than older men in the population.

Overall unemployment rates have fallen for both sexes, but particularly for men, since the early 1990s (Figure 18).

Age differences in economic inactivity and unemployment

Economic inactivity is, not surprisingly, highest for those aged over 60, followed by those aged over 50 and 16–17-year-olds

Young adults are particularly affected by unemployment. While the rate for 18- to 24-year-olds has fallen by a third over the last decade, most of the fall had been achieved by 1999; there are still half a million young unemployed and their rate is still two-and-a-half times that for older workers, which has halved during the same period (Poverty.org.uk). Unemployment rates for 18- to 24-year-olds in Wales and the North East are double the rates in the South East (excluding London).

Workless households (households where at least one person is of working age but no one is in employment)

In 2004, there were around two and three-quarter million (around 16 per cent) workless working-age households compared with 3 million in 1994. Two-thirds of all workless working-age households are single adult households, with a quarter of these being lone parents and the other three-quarters single adults without dependent children.

The rate of worklessness for lone parent households with dependent children was 42 per cent in spring 2004 – 1 per cent lower than in the previous year and 8 per cent below the rate in spring 1997.

Figure 18: **Unemployment, by sex, United Kingdom, 1984–2004**

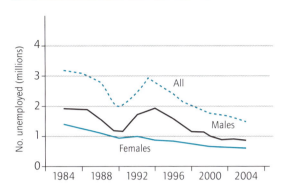

Source: *Social Trends*, 2005

Figure 19: **Workless households, by household composition, United Kingdom, 1998–2003**

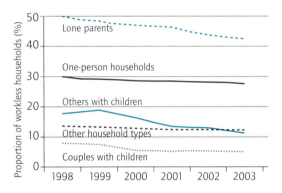

Source: Babb *et al*, 2004

The rate of worklessness for couple-households with dependent children was 5 per cent, 2 per cent lower than in spring 1997.

Seventeen per cent of households with one full-time worker have low income and over a third of all low-income households have someone working. (Babb *et al*, 2004) (Figure 19).

Factors involved in unemployment/ economic inactivity

Disadvantage

Those most at risk of non-employment are:

- lone parents,
- disabled people,
- people with low or no qualifications and skills,
- people aged over 50,
- people living in the most deprived areas,
- members of (some) minority ethnic groups.

Table 27 shows that unemployment has declined among all these groups in the last decade. However, they remain around twice as likely to be unemployed as other people of working-age.

Belonging to a minority ethnic group

People of Bangladeshi, African, Pakistani and Caribbean descent are twice as likely as white people to be out of work but wanting work. People of Chinese origin on the other hand have much lower non-employment rates (Figure 20).

Table 27: **Unemployment rates[a] of disadvantaged groups, United Kingdom, 1994–2003**

	1994	1999	2003
		(%)	
Older people[b]	9	5	3
30 LAs[c]	15	12	9
Minority ethnic group	21	13	11
Lone parents	18	15	10
Low qualifications[d]	16	12	10
Disabled	–	11	8
All	10	6	5

a Unemployment rates for working age people, men aged 16–64 and women aged 16–59. Spring quarters. Data are not Census adjusted.
b Those aged 50 to 64 for men and 50–59 for women
c People living in the 30 local authority districts with the poorest initial labour market position
d Those with no formal qualifications

Source: Babb *et al*, 2004

Figure 20: **Inactivity rates, by ethnic background, United Kingdom, 2004**

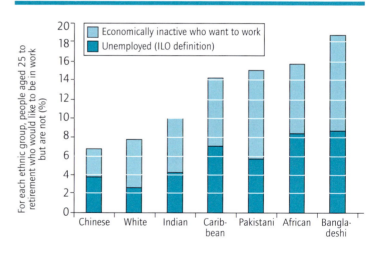

Source: Poverty.org.uk

No or low qualification

In Spring 2004, 31 per cent of the economically inactive and 20 per cent of the unemployed had no qualifications, compared to 9 per cent of employees and 13 per cent of the self-employed (Figure 21).

Sickness or disability

Long-term sickness or disability is the most common reason given for economic inactivity by working-age men, particularly for those aged 35 to 49 (60 per cent) (*Social Trends*, 2005) (Table 28).

Domestic and caring responsibilities

For working-age women the most common reason given for economic inactivity is looking after the family or home. In 2004, 45 per cent said this was their main reason for not seeking work. This rose to 72 per cent of 25- to 34-year-olds – the cohort most likely to have dependent children (*Social Trends*, 2005) (Table 28).

The Department for Work and Pensions' (DWP) has a Public Service Agreement (PSA) target 'to increase the employment rates of disadvantaged areas and groups, taking account of the economic cycle'. The key target groups are people with disabilities, lone parents, minority ethnic groups, people aged over 50, those with the lowest qualifications and people living in the 30 UK local authority districts with the poorest initial labour market position. The government's intention is to reduce the difference between their employment rates and the overall, national rate (Treasury and DWP, 2003).

Figure 21: **Unemployed according to level of qualification, United Kingdom, 2004**

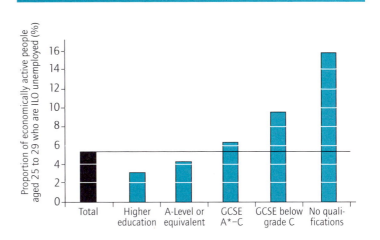

Source: Poverty.org.uk

Table 28: **Reasons for economic activity by sex and age, United Kingdom, 2004**

	16–24	25–34	35–49	50–59/64	All aged 16–59/64
			(%)		
Males					
Long-term sick or disabled	5	38	60	53	37
Looking after family or home	1	12	17	4	6
Student	84	25	4	–	30
Retired	0	0	–	31	13
Other	10	26	18	12	14
All males	100	100	100	100	100
Females					
Long-term sick or disabled	4	10	24	42	21
Looking after family or home	22	72	59	27	45
Student	64	8	4	1	19
Retired	0	0	–	15	4
Other	10	10	11	16	12
All females	100	100	100	100	100

Source: *Social Trends*, 2005

2.4 Earnings

Between April 2002 and April 2003, the average gross weekly pay of full-time employees in Great Britain increased by 2.4 per cent to £476 compared with the growth in prices as measured by the UK retail prices index (RPI) of 3.1 per cent, indicating a real terms fall in earnings (*Social Trends*, 2005).

Earning differentials

By sector

The lowest pay rates are in the public sector followed by the wholesale and retail sector. Almost a third of employees aged over 25 in the public sector earn less than £6.50 an hour (Poverty.org.uk). More than half of employees on below-average incomes are not contributing to a non-state pension.

The number of younger workers aged 18–21 on low pay (at or below full adult minimum wage) has remained largely unchanged since 1998.

By employee qualification level

Employees with no qualifications earn the lowest hourly wage (around £6 per hour) compared with those with a Level 4 qualification or higher (usually a university degree or higher) earning around £15.50 per hour. Figure 22 illustrates the difference in earnings between those with higher and lower qualifications

Figure 23 shows that these earning differentials tend to persist throughout working life. Especially at age 35–44 and over 55.

Half of all 24- to 29-year-old employees with no qualifications earn less than £200 per week. This compares with a third of those with GCSEs but without NVQ2 or equivalent, and a sixth of those with NVQ2 or better qualifications (Poverty.org.uk).

Figure 22: **Earnings related to level of highest qualification, United Kingdom, Spring 2003**

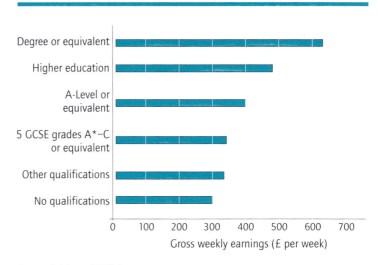

Source: Babb *et al*, 2004

Figure 23: **Pay related to qualification, by age, United Kingdom, 2004**

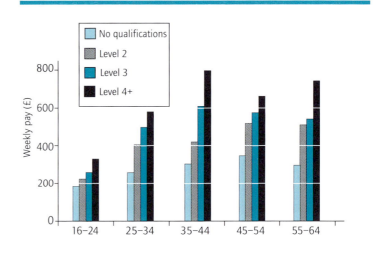

By sex

Women earn less than men at all levels of qualification. Table 29 shows that part of the discrepancy results from their stereotypical occupational patterns. Many of the lowest-paid jobs are in employment sectors dominated by women, and the highest in sectors dominated by men.

2.5 Benefit claimants

At August 2004, there were 4,483,000 claimants of key benefits of working age (the main benefits claimed for unemployment, sickness or disability, for lone parents on benefit, and other Income Support claimants). This number has fallen by 964,000 since May 1997.

Claimants of Jobcentre Plus benefits

The total number of working-age people depending on Jobcentre Plus-administered benefits has fallen by 1,178,000 since May 1997. Table 30 shows the numbers of adults depending on these benefits in May and August 2004. By far the largest group of claimants were those with sickness or disability.

While the overall number of people claiming Jobcentre Plus benefits has started to fall, there has been an increase in the number of women claiming sickness and disability benefits. Between May 2001 and August 2004, the number of women claiming sickness and disability benefits rose by 4.2 per cent, compared with a fall for men of 1.5 per cent.

Regional differences

The proportion of the working-age population on Jobcentre Plus benefits ranges from 8.6 per cent in the South East to 18.4 per cent in the North East.

The biggest variation is in the numbers and proportion on sickness and disability benefits – varying from 13.1 per cent of the population in Wales to 5.4 per cent in the South East.

In some areas – mainly those with the highest employment rates – claims can be in low single percentage point figures. In other areas, such as parts of South Wales, and in the North West and

Table 29: **Reasons for economic activity by sex and age, United Kingdom, 2004**

	Median gross weekly pay
Highest paid	
Directors and chief executives of major organisations	1,791
Senior officials in national government	1,687
Medical practitioners	1,168
Aircraft pilots and flight engineers	1,094
Financial managers and chartered secretaries	951
Solicitors and lawyers, judges and coroners	832
Police officers (inspectors and above)	825
Managers in mining and energy	819
IT strategy and planning professionals	795
Lowest paid	
Hairdressers, barbers	219
School mid-day assistants	218
Kitchen and catering assistants	216
Bar staff	213
Waiters, waitresses	206
Retail cashiers and check-out operators	204
Elementary personal services occupations[a]	204
Launderers, dry cleaners, pressers	204
Floral arrangers,. florists	197
Leisure and theme park attendants	191

a Not elsewhere classified

Source: Humphreys, 2005

Table 30: **Adults depending on Jobcentre Plus benefits, Great Britain, May 2004**

	Benefit recipients	% of recipients	Annual change	% of population of working age
Unemployed	775,000	14.7	−92,000	2.2
Sick and disabled (excluding DLA only)	2,729,000	51.8	−10,000	7.6
Lone parents	783,000	14.9	−40,000	2.2
Other IS claimants	196,000	3.7	4,000	0.5
All claimants	4,483,000	85.1	−138,000	12.5
Partners	785,000	14.9	−28,0001	2.2
All working age	5,268,000	100	−166,000	14.7
Children	2,694,000	−	−129,000[a]	21

a Numbers of partners and children restated at a higher level due to increased eligibility following the introduction of new Tax Credits. (Source: *Working Brief*, March, 2005)
DLA (Disability Living Allowance); IS (Income Support)

Source: *Working Brief*, 162, March 2005

North East, up to one-third of the local working-age population are claiming Incapacity Benefit (*Working Brief*, 2005a).

For children, the proportions supported by Jobcentre Plus benefits vary from 29 per cent over the whole of London, to 14 per cent in the South East (*Working Brief*, 2005c).

2.6 Government employment programmes: participation and results

In the UK there are several government programmes which aspire to increase the numbers of working age people in employment.

Changes to national programmes and initiatives for those not in work

Pathways to Work

The *Pathways to Work* pilots for those on Incapacity Benefit (IB) have been extended to those who have been on IB for a long period of time and will eventually become a national offer.

The extension of help to long-term claimants includes:

- A £20 a week Job Preparation Premium to encourage steps towards getting a job.
- Compulsory work-focused interviews with specially trained Personal Advisers.
- Access to NHS rehabilitation support or other employment programmes.
- A £40-a-week Return to Work Credit when they get a job.

Incapacity Benefit

The expression ' Incapacity Benefit' will no longer be used.

Two new benefits 'Rehabilitation Support Allowance' and 'Disability Sickness Allowance' will differentiate between those who have a severe condition and those with potentially more manageable conditions

Figure 24a: **New Deal for Young People, United Kingdom, 1998–2005**

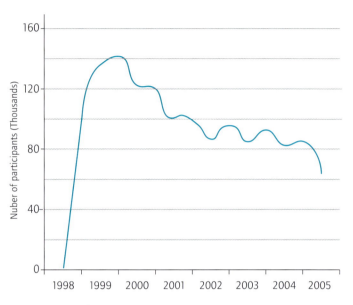

Source: DWP, 2005b

Figure 24b: **Young people into employment, United Kingdom, 1998–2004**

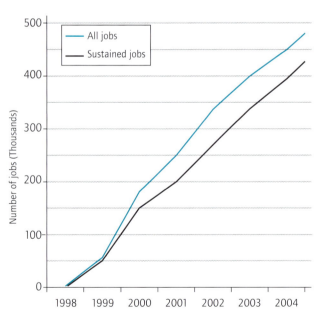

Source: DWP, 2005b

Initially, people will be put on a holding benefit paid at JSA (Jobseekers Allowance) rates, accessing the new reformed benefits only once they have been through a proper medical assessment within 12 weeks (*Working Brief*, 2005c).

Pathways to Work for lone parents

The Pathways to Work for Lone Parents is intended to give more choice and more help to lone parents to enable them to move off welfare and into work.

The help will include extra support and childcare and Work Credit will be extended to give those moving into work £40 a week in addition to other benefits The package is being piloted in five areas and is designed to help the government towards their goal to achieve 70 per cent of lone parents in employment (Figure 25).

Figure 25a: **New Deal for Lone Parents, United Kingdom, 1998–2004**

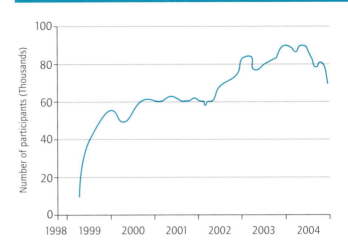

Source: DWP, 2005b

Figure 25b: **Lone parents into employment, United Kingdom, 1998–2004**

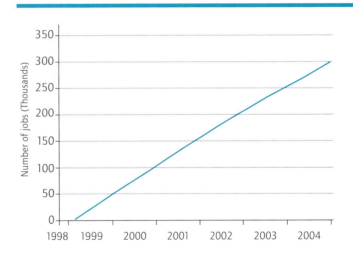

Source: DWP, 2005b

Figure 26a: **New Deal for Long-Term Unemployed People 25+, United Kingdom, 1998–2004**

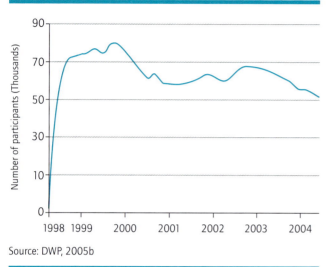

Source: DWP, 2005b

Figure 27a: **Employment Zones, United Kingdom, 2000–2004**

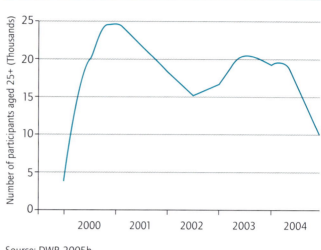

Source: DWP, 2005b

Figure 26b: **Long-term unemployed people aged 25+ into employment, United Kingdom, 1998–2004**

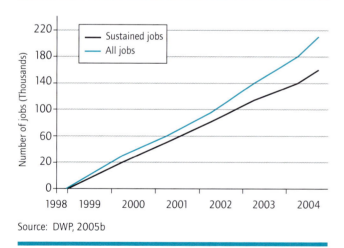

Source: DWP, 2005b

Figure 27b: **Employment Zones: participants into employment, aged 25+, United Kingdom, 2000–2004**

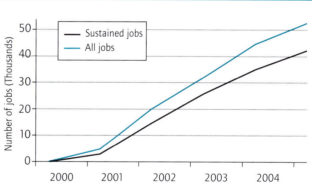

Source: DWP, 2005b

Figure 28a: **New Deal for Disabled People, United Kingdom, 2001–04**

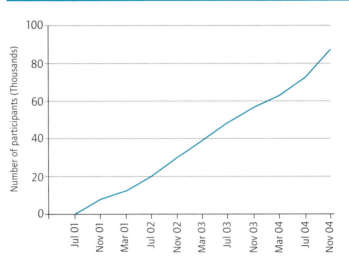

Source: DWP, 2005b

Figure 28b: **New Deal for Disabled People into employment, United Kingdom, 2002–04**

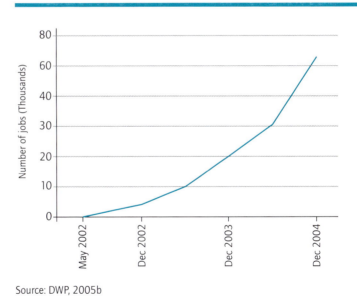

Source: DWP, 2005b

Figure 29: **New Deal 50+, United Kingdom, 2003–04**

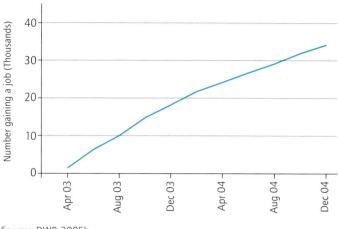

Source: DWP, 2005b

Figure 30a: **Work-Based Learning for Adults, England, 2001–04**

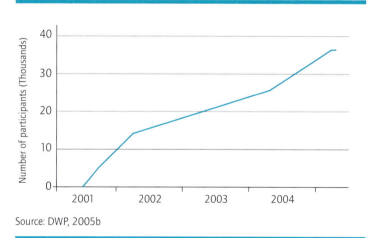

Source: DWP, 2005b

Figure 30b: **Work-Based Learning for Adults into Employment, England, 2001–04**

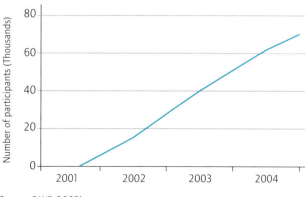

Source: DWP, 2005b

2.7 Employment and skill gaps

Increases and improvements in the skills of the workforce are a priority for the current government. This is demonstrated by the Skills Strategy White Papers (DfES, 2003a and 2005a), the setting up of the sector skills councils and regional skills partnerships, and the stated priorities for post-16 education, as reflected in the LSC 's annual statement of priorities *The Skills We Need*, published in December 2004:

- To make learning truly demand led.
- To ensure that all 14–19 year-olds have access to quality learning.
- To transform FE so that it attracts business investment in skills training.
- To strengthen {the LSC) role in regional regeneration.
- To extend (the LSC) influence on economic development and job creation.
- To improve the skills of workers in the public sector.
  (LSC, 2004a)

These priorities are based on concerns about the UK's lower levels of productivity compared with that of some of its main competitors (Figure 31).

The government's aim is to remedy the employment gaps and skills shortages that have been identified in the labour market and to bring the UK up to the level of its nearest competitors.

Recruitment gaps

The annual Recruitment, Retention and Turnover Survey conducted by the Chartered Institute of Personnel and Development (CIPD, 2005) found that 85 per cent of firms had experienced difficulty in recruiting staff over the previous year: 45 per cent said that the most difficult vacancies to fill were management and professional vacancies.

Recruitment problems can be disproportionately high or low in relation to the distribution of employment. In 2003 recruitment problems were disproportionately high for transport operatives, caring personal service occupations and among business associate professionals (LSC, 2005a).

Figure 31: **Productivity comparisons**

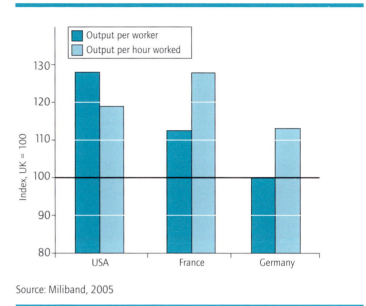

Source: Miliband, 2005

Figure 32: **Skills shortages, by sector, United Kingdom, 2003**

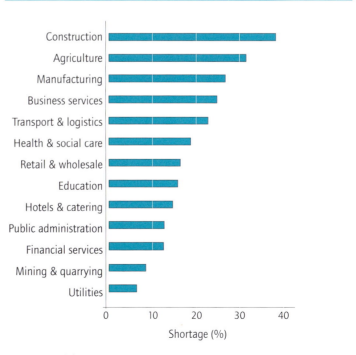

Source: Humphries, 2005

According to The National Employers' 2003 Skills Survey (NESS), health care and social work had the highest number of vacancies (13.3 per cent) of all the industry sectors surveyed in the UK. Of these vacancies, 19.2 per cent were reported to be a result of skills shortages (Hogarth *et al*, 2005).

There were also recruitment problem for many skilled trades and associate professional occupations including construction. It has been estimated that:

● The construction industry will need 415,800 new people to join between 2003 and 2007 – a total of 83,160 each year.

● The most in-demand occupations will be carpenters and joiners (11,910 needed per year); managers (9,770); bricklayers (5,880); technicians (2,230) and plumbers (6,280). In addition, 4,950 professionals will also be needed per year. (CIPD, 2004)

Many of these occupations are highly segregated by sex, and recruitment problems in these areas may be related to the difficulties of attracting women into such jobs (LSC, 2005a).

Skill shortages

Skills audits indicate that the UK is lacking in supply of technical skills (often sector-specific) as well as certain generic skills. These vary between occupational areas. The National Employer Skills Survey (NESS) 2003 found that two occupational categories had a larger share of skills gaps than they did of employment gaps:

● Sales and customer service occupations (19 per cent of all skills gaps compared with 16 per cent of total employment), and

● Elementary occupations (16 per cent of all skills gaps compared with 14 per cent of total employment).
(Hogarth *et al*, 2005).

Figures 32–34 indicate economic sectors and occupations where skills shortages are located, and where shortages are particularly acute.

Figure 33 shows that soft skills as well as technical skills are in demand. The LSC report *Skills in*

England 2004 highlights the need for customer, communication and information-handling skills at all levels as well as the continuing need for ICT skills, technical and practical skills (LSC, 2005a).

Figure 33: **Skills shortages, by occupation, United Kingdom, 2003**

Source: Humphries, 2005

Figure 34: **Skills in particularly short supply, United Kingdom, 2003**

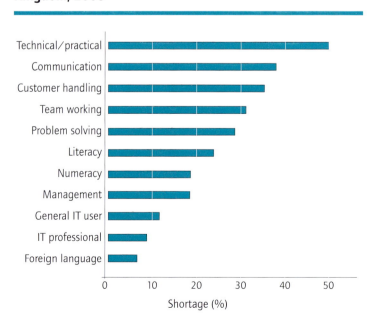

Source: Humphries, 2005.

Skills policies

Based on information from Hogarth *et al* (2004) – the National Employers' Skills Survey – the LSC stresses the importance of supplying skills in areas of rapidly growing demand and replacing those leaving the workforce in certain key areas, even where employment is expected to decline.

The policy aims to:
- Increase young people's progression into further education and training including apprenticeships.
- Increase employer engagement, for example through the Sector Skills Councils, Regional Skills Partnerships and Employer Training Pilots.
- Concentrate resources for adults on education and training that improves basic skills (Skills for Life) and qualifications (the Level 2 learning entitlement).

The 2005–08 Public Sector Agreement (PSA) targets for DfES include:
- That young people be ready for skilled employment or higher education by age 19, with substantial increases in full Level 2 achievement from 14 to19 and participation at age 17 increasing from 75 per cent to 90 per cent over the next 10 years.
- An increase to 28 per cent, by July 2005, in the proportion of young people entering an apprenticeship before the age of 22.
- An increase by 75 per cent, between 2002–03 and 2007–08, in the numbers successfully completing apprenticeships as the main work-based route for young people to gain employment skills.
- 2.25 million adults to achieve functional competence in literacy, language and numeracy, and over three million adults to achieve a first full Level 2 qualification by 2010.
- An agreed framework of shared priorities that link skills and qualifications to improved business performance and labour market capacity.

The National Employer Training Programme (NETP) is to be the key delivery mechanism to raise the numbers of people with Level 3 from 2006–07, with two regions piloting a matched funding system between employers and government to deliver Level 3 qualifications

Sector Skills Councils are charged with shaping the supply of skills from further and higher education to meet employer and employee needs, and are to act as a medium through which employers gain leverage over training.

The main mechanisms for raising adult skills are the commitment to free skills for life (literacy, language and numeracy), and a entitlement to free learning to gain a full level 2 for adults who lack this level of qualification.

The next section examines current levels of attainment in the population.

Section 3
Educational attainment

3.1 International comparisons

Over the last ten years there has been a significant improvement in overall qualification levels in the UK, including a rise in those educated to Levels 3, 4 and 5, and a drop in the proportion of the population who are without qualifications.

The UK comes 13th out of 30 OECD countries in a ranking of the proportion of the population aged 55 to 64 who have achieved upper-secondary education, but 22nd for those aged 25 to 34. However, the UK is now above the OECD average in relation to the proportion of the workforce qualified to NVQ Level 4 and above, and has one of the highest rates of university graduation (OECD, 2004b).

The proportion of people aged 19–21 in the UK with qualifications at Level 2 and above is higher than in Germany and the USA but significantly lower than in France. At Level 3 and above, the proportions are similar in all four countries. For those aged 25–28, the UK lags behind France and Germany, especially at Level 3 and above (LSC, 2004a). In France and Germany, vocational qualifications contribute considerably towards raising the qualifications of young people (Centre for Economic Performance, 2004).

3.2 Government policies and targets

In the UK, qualifications are used as a proxy for skills: a major preoccupation of government is to raise qualification levels in the population.

The Skills Strategy, launched in 2003 (DfES, 2003a) aims to tackle the skills gap between the UK and its main economic competitors. One of the main mechanisms for achieving the goals identified and increasing people's employability in England is the introduction of a Level 2 entitlement, an initiative whereby adults can learn to obtain their first full Level 2 qualification free of charge.

Qualifications equivalent to a full Level 2 are:
- 5 GCSEs grade A–C (or 5 O-levels):
- NVQ Level 2
- BTEC, SCOTVEC first or general diploma
- Edexcel first diploma
- GNVQ Intermediate
- City & Guilds Craft/part 2
- RSA Diploma
- 2 AS-levels
- 1 A-level
- SCE Higher (1 or 2)
- Intermediate 2 Higher qualification

The Adult Learning Grant provides weekly support to adults studying full time for first Level 2 qualification, and for young adults studying for first Level 3 qualification.

The Adult Learning Grant pilots started in 10 pilot areas in 2003, with 86 colleges and further education providers involved. By February 2004, more than 2 700 applications had been received, and £500 000 in Adult Learning Grants paid to learners.

3.3 Attainment of different qualifications

GCSEs

In Summer 2004:

- 53 per cent of 16-year-olds in England achieved at least five GCSEs at grades A*–C and 86 per cent gained at least five GCSEs at grades A*–G (the national Learning Target is 92 per cent).

- In Wales, 51 per cent of 15-year-olds gained at least five GCSEs at grades A*–C (target 58 per cent) and 85 per cent of 15-year-olds gained at least five GCSEs at grades A*–G (target 95 per cent).

A-Levels or equivalent

- 38.5 per cent of young people in the United Kingdom achieved two or more GCE A-level passes or equivalent in schools and FE colleges in 2002–03.

- Most frequently studied subjects at A-level/ Higher Grade were English Language, English Literature, Social Studies, Mathematics, Biological Sciences and General Studies.

- Of the 77,200 VCE A/AS and Double Award qualifications obtained in England, Wales and Northern Ireland in 2002–03, the most frequent subject areas were Information Technology and

Business

In 2003–04:

- 92 per cent of A-level candidates aged 16–18 achieved two or more GCE/VCE A-level (or equivalent) passes.

- 9 per cent of A-level candidates achieved three or more A grades – a steady rise since 1994–95.

GNVQs

Of the 138,400 Intermediate and Foundation GNVQ entries in England, Wales and Northern Ireland in 2002–03, 42 per cent achieved GNVQ Part One, and 27 per cent achieved a Full GNVQ. Of the VCE A/AS and Double Award passes in 2002–03. 33,100 were Double Awards, 31,600 were A-level and 12,500 were AS passes (DfES, 2004a).

Full Vocational Awards

432,000 NVQs were awarded in the United Kingdom in 2002–03. Almost three-fifths were awarded at Level 2. Some 217,000 vocationally related qualifications were awarded in 2002–03, with 45 per cent of these awarded at Level 1.

Figure 35: **GCSE results, by region, England and Wales, 2002–03**

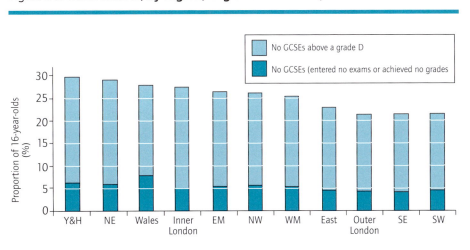

Source: Poverty.org.uk, Education graphs

Higher education qualifications

A total of 511,500 higher education qualifications were awarded in higher education institutions in the United Kingdom in 2002–03. Of these, 94,400 were sub-degree qualifications, 273,400 were first degrees, 11,800 were PhD or equivalents and 131,900 were at Masters/other postgraduate level.

3.4 Highest qualifications held

In Spring 2004:

- 45 per cent of people of working age in the UK were qualified to NVQ Level 3 equivalent or above, and 26 per cent to NVQ Level 4 equivalent or above.
- The number of people in England with Level 5 has more than doubled in a decade although this still represents just under 6 per cent of the economically active population.

Table 31 shows that men have slightly higher qualifications levels than women at the upper levels and that younger people have higher qualifications than those aged over 40.

Table 31: **Highest qualifications held by people of working age,[a] by sex, age and ethnic origin, United Kingdom, 2004**

| | All people of working age[a] | | | Proportion of people of working age | | | |
		NVQ Level 5[b]	NVQ Level 4[c]	NVQ Level 3[d]	NVQ Level 2[d]	Below NVQ Level 2[d]	No qualifications
	(Thousands)				(%)		
By sex							
Male	18,622	6	21	23	21	16	14
Female	17,657	5	21	15	22	20	16
By age							
16–19	3,045	–	1	21	36	21	21
20–24	3,613	2	18	34	22	16	8
25–29	3,543	6	31	19	19	16	8
30–39	8,786	7	25	16	21	21	10
40–49	8,307	6	23	17	19	16	24
50–64	8,985	5	20	17	19	16	24
By ethnic origin							
White	33,078	5	21	20	22	18	15
Non-white	3,182	6	19	16	21	20	19
of which:							
Mixed	264	6	22	23	22	15	12
Asian or Asian British	1,562	6	18	15	20	19	23
Black or black British	792	5	20	17	22	22	14
Chinese	154	12	21	15	17	20	15
Other ethnic group	410	8	18	11	20	23	20

a Working age is defined as males aged 16–64 and females 16–59. These figures include unpaid family workers, those on government employment training programmes, or those who did not answer, who are excluded from the economic activity analyses below.
b Includes higher degrees and other qualifications at Level 5
c Includes first degree and other degrees and sub-degree higher education qualifications.
d Vocational and academic.

Source: DfES, 2004b

Figure 36: **High and low qualifications, by region, United Kingdom, 2004**

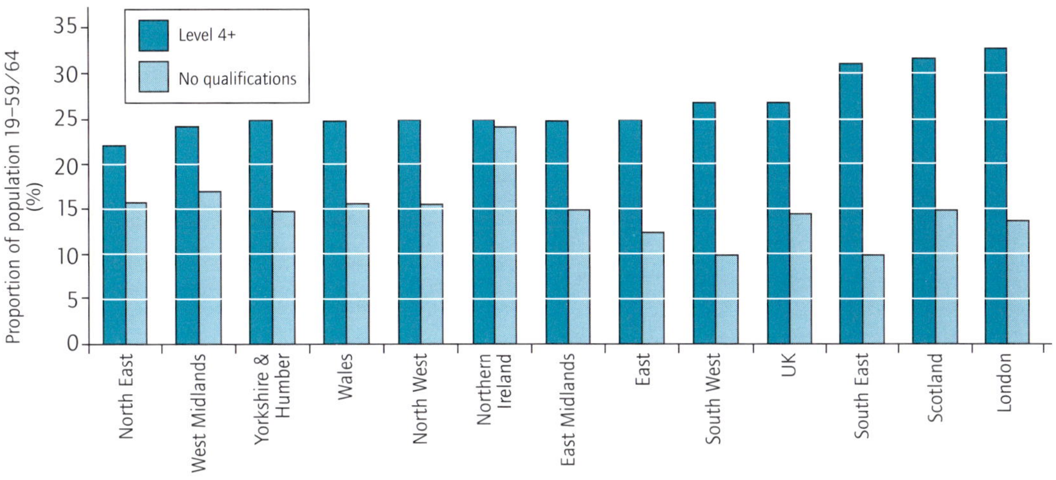

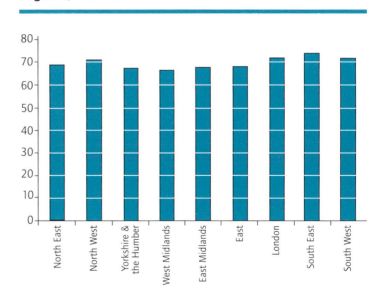

Source: *Labour Force Survey UK*, Spring, 2004

3.5 Highest qualification by region

Attainment levels vary by Government Office region (Figure 36). In Spring 2004:

- London had a higher proportion of highly qualified people (i.e. qualified to NVQ Level 4 and 5 or equivalent) than any other UK region, closely followed by Scotland and the South East.

3.6 Level 2 achievement

In 2004, 70.2 per cent of economically active adults in England (males aged 18 to 64 and females aged 18 to 59) had attained at least NVQ Level 2 or equivalents (Figure 37).

For Wales, 64.6 per cent of economically active adults had attained at least NVQ Level 2 or equivalents in 2003. The highest proportion was 73 per cent for Ceredigion and the lowest, 46.8 per cent, in Blaenau Gwent.

Figure 37: **Proportion of economically active who had attained at least NVQ Level 2 or equivalent, by region, England, 2003–04**

Source: *Annual Local Area Labour Force Survey*, 2003–04

43 per cent of working-age adults held an NVQ Level 3 or above and 24 per cent were qualified to Level 4 or above (Table 32),

For Scotland, 67.9 per cent of economically active adults had attained at least Level 2 or equivalent in 2003. The highest proportion was 82.4 per cent for East Renfrewshire and the lowest proportion, 60.0 per cent in North Lanarkshire. Table 33 shows how the level of qualification in Scotland tends to decline for those aged over 34 except among those with professional qualifications, the largest proportion of whom are aged 45–59.

Table 32: **Levels of highest qualifications held by working age adults, by age group and sex, Wales, 2003**

	18–24	25–34	35–49	50–59	All of working age
			(%)		
No qualifications					
Male	8.0	10.7	14.6	20.3	15.6
Female	9.2	12.8	19.1	31.4	19.1
All	8.6	11.8	16.9	25.8	17.3
Level 2 or higher					
Male	74.8	71.3	68.0	66.8	68.5
Female	77.2	65.5	59.1	50.2	61.2
All	76.0	68.3	63.5	58.5	64.9
Level 3 or higher					
Male	49.0	51.2	47.2	46.4	47.3
Female	52.5	44.1	36.7	30.9	39.4
All	50.8	47.5	41.8	38.6	43.4
Level 4 or higher					
Male	13.8	30.5	25.5	23.3	23.6
Female	17.9	29.7	26.0	22.5	24.7
All	15.9	30.1	25.7	22.9	24.2

Source: National Assembly for Wales, 2005

Table 33: **Qualifications held, by age and by sex, Scotland, 2003**

	16–24	25–34	35–44	45–59	60–64	All of working age
			(%)			
No qualifications						
Male						19
Female						22
All	8	11	17	28	39	20
'O' Grade or equivalent						
Male						67
Female						68
All	84	80	71	58	48	67
Highers or equivalent						
Male						60
Female						51
All	63	65	59	50	34	55
First or higher degree						
Male						17
Female						15
All	11	24	18	14	9	15
Professional qualifications						
Male						14
Female						15
All	3	14	16	18	16	16
Base	1,000	2,057	2,632	3,260	1,089	(M) 4,438 (F) 5,600 (All)10,038

Note: Columns add to more than 100% since multiple responses were allowed.

Source: Scottish Executive, 2003

3.7 Staying-on rates in England

Figures drawn from the Poverty.org website show that the number of school-leavers training in England not in education or training remained the same, nearly 17 per cent, between 2000 and 2004.

3.8 Low or no qualifications

Among the population as a whole

Between 1997 and 2003 the number of people in the UK qualified below Level 2 or with no qualifications declined in contrast to the better-qualified.

In Spring 2004 15 per cent of people of working age in the UK had no qualification. There are small differences between different countries

- In England in 2004, 14 per cent of working age men and 16 per cent of women had no qualifications (Labour Force Survey, Spring 2004).
- In Wales in 2003, 13 per cent of people of working age had no qualification. (National Assembly for Wales, 2005).
- In Scotland, in 2003, 17 per cent of people of working age had no qualification – a fall for the second successive year (Scottish Executive, 2005).

Figure 38 shows sex and ethnic differences: people of Pakistani and Bangladeshi origin have particularly high rates of non-qualification in 2002–03.

Among young adults

12 per cent of 16-year-olds in England and Wales failed to obtain five or more GCSEs in 2004 and 6 per cent obtained no GCSEs at all. These proportions are the same as in 2000.

While the proportion of 16-year-olds gaining only low grades in their GCSEs has been declining throughout the last decade, 25 per cent still obtain no GCSEs above a grade D (New Policy Institute, 2005).

Figure 38: **No qualifications,[a] by ethnic group and sex, Great Britain, 2002–03**

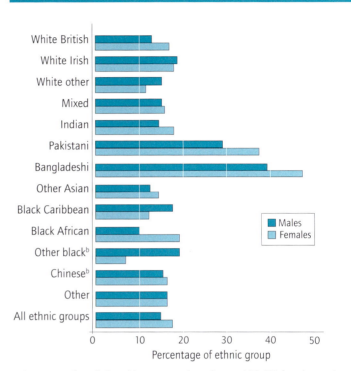

Percentage of ethnic group

a As a proportion of all working age people: males aged 16–64, females aged 16–59.
b The number of respondents for males and femlaes in the 'Other black' ethnic group is very small. The same applies for the males in the Chinese ethnic group. Therefore the figures for these groups are only indicative.

Source: *Annual Local Area Labour Force Survey*, 2003–04

There are some regional differences in England, with noticeably poorer GCSE results in the North East and Yorkshire and the Humber than in the South (Figure 35).

Almost 30 per cent of all 19-year-olds in the UK lacked an NVQ Level 2 or equivalent in 2004. This proportion has been rising since 2001 after falling steadily during the second half of the 1990s. One in twelve have no qualifications at all.

Figure 39 shows the number of 19-year-olds in the UK with low or no qualifications from 1996–97 to 2003–04.

3.9 Low levels of literary, language and numeracy

Basic skill deficiencies are still causing national concern. A survey in England has suggested that about 5 per cent of adults of working have literacy skills below Entry Level 3, that 16 per cent fall below Level 1, and that 21 per cent have numeracy skills below Entry Level 3 and 47 per cent below Level 1; the North East had the lowest results of any region. (DfES, 2003).

In spring 2005, 26 million people in England were deemed to lack the literacy and numeracy skills expected of school leavers. (http://senet.lsc. gov. uk/guide2/skillsforlife/index.cfm).

A survey in Wales suggested that a higher proportion of adults than in England have literacy at Entry Level or below Level 1 (25 per cent) and numeracy skills below Level 1 (53 per cent) (Williams and Kinnaird, 2004).

Figure 39: **19-year-olds with low or no qualifications, United Kingdom, 1996–2004**

Source: Poverty.org website

Table 34: **Highest qualification, by age[a] and sex, Great Britain, 2003–04**

	Degree or equivalent	Higher education qualification[b]	GCE A-Level or equivalent	GCSE grades A*–C or equivalent	Other qualification	No qualification
			(%)			
Males						
16–19	–	–	28	42	11	17
20–24	14	6	38	22	12	7
25–29	29	8	23	17	14	8
30–39	22	9	25	19	15	9
40–49	20	9	30	15	13	12
50–64	17	9	32	10	13	20
All males	18	8	29	18	13	13
Females						
16–19	–	1	31	45	8	13
20–24	16	7	35	24	9	8
25–29	29	9	20	21	12	8
30–39	20	10	16	29	14	11
40–49	17	12	15	27	14	16
50–59	11	12	12	20	18	28
All females	16	10	18	27	14	15

a Males aged 16 to 64, females aged 16 to 59.
b Below degree level.

Source: *Social Trends*, 2005

3.10 Sex differences in attainment

Men tend to be more highly qualified than women overall.

Approximately 49 per cent of men of working age have qualifications at Level 3 or above, compared to 40 per cent of women. Fifty-three per cent of economically active men are qualified to Level 3 or above compared to 47 per cent of women (DfES, 2004a) (Table 34). In winter 2003–04, 18 per cent of working-age men, and 16 per cent of working-age women had a degree or equivalent.

The difference is mainly due to an age factor. Those aged 50 and over are the most likely to hold no qualifications, and there are more women in this group than men. The proportion of men aged 50 to 64 with a degree or equivalent is one-and-a-half times that of women aged 50 to 59 (DfES, 2004a) (Table 34).

Looking at the younger cohorts, however, it is clear that women are rapidly catching up with men in terms of overall qualification levels:
- More young women stay on in post-16 education and training than young men. In 2003, 26 per cent of male students aged 16–28 did not participate in education or training compared to 24 per cent of females (DfES, 2005f).
- Girls continue to out-perform boys at GCSE level. About 60 per cent of girls gain 5 or more GCSEs at grades A–C, compared to 47 per cent of boys (DfES, 2005b). In England, the sex difference applies across all ethnic groups, with Chinese and Indian pupils acquiring particularly good grades (Figure 40).
- In 2003–04, 132,100 female students aged 16–18 achieved 2+ A-levels or equivalent, compared to 112,100 males (DfES, 2005c).
- 12.3 per cent of women aged between 16 and 24 hold higher-level qualifications (Level 4+) compared to 10.6 per cent of men (Labour Force Survey, Spring 2004).

In 2002–03 in the UK, 57 per cent of all higher education qualifications were awarded to women.

3.11 Subject variations

There are still some sex differences in attainment according to subject.

In 2003–04 girls outperformed boys in all the most common subjects studied at GCSE level (Table 34). Of the selected subjects shown, the biggest difference in the proportions of entrants achieving grades A*–C (20 percentage points) was in art and design, for which 77 per cent of girls who entered for the exam achieved a high grade compared to 58 per cent of boys. Other high differentials were in English (language and literature), design and technology, French, and German.

The smallest difference in attainment (2 percentage points) was in mathematics: around half of boys and girls who took the exam achieved a grade A*–C. Even when more boys than girls entered for an exam, for example design and technology, a smaller proportion of boys than girls achieved a grade

Figure 40: **Achievement of five or more GCSEs grades A*–C/ GNVQs, by sex and ethnic group, England, 2003**

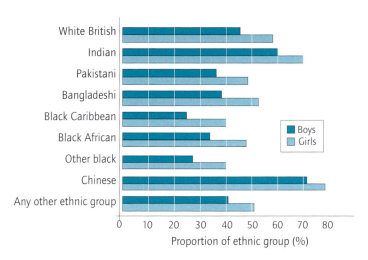

Source: Babb *et al*, 2004

A*–C. This pattern was consistent across commonly studied subjects where male entrants outnumbered female entrants (*Social Trends*, 2005). It was apparent in every ethnic group (Figure 40).

Table 35: **GCSE or equivalent entries and achievements, by subject and sex, United Kingdom, 2002–03**

	Number of entries (Thousands)			Percentage of entrants achieving grade A*–C		
	Males	Females	All	Males	Females	All
Mathematics	371	362	733	51	53	52
English	348	347	696	54	69	62
English Literature[a]	269	287	555	58	73	66
Science Double Award	261	266	527	53	56	55
Design and Technology	252	215	467	47	63	54
French	171	194	365	43	59	52
Geography	137	107	245	59	66	62
History	119	119	237	61	68	64
Art and Design	96	132	228	58	77	69
Physical Education	93	46	139	58	62	60
German	66	71	138	49	62	56
Information Technology	70	47	117	57	64	60
Science Single Award	40	38	78	18	21	20

a Data are for England and Wales only.

Source: *Social Trends*, 2005

In Scotland the differences in attainment between the sexes are not so great. In 2002–03, female students leaving publicly-funded schools received a higher number of school-leaving qualifications in a number of subjects but boys outperformed girls in mathematics, physics, computing studies, graphic communication, technological studies and information systems (Table 36).

There are also sex differences in A-level results. Table 37 for 2003–04 shows that a higher proportion of young women achieve more A grades than young men in virtually all subjects including maths and the sciences.

Section 4 presents data on post-16 participation patterns.

Table 36: **Total qualifications attained by leavers from publicly funded schools at SCQF level 7, by subject and sex, Scotland, 2003–04**

	Males	Females	Total	Percentage of all leavers
Total leavers	29,985	28,426	58,411	100
Mathematics	813	599	1,412	2.4
Chemistry	501	549	1,050	1.8
Biology	227	665	892	1.5
Physics	680	190	870	1.5
English	224	579	803	1.4
Art and Design	184	508	692	1.2
Music	216	323	539	0.9
Geography	245	277	522	0.9
History	208	287	495	0.8
Modern Studies	125	253	378	0.6
French	54	276	330	0.6
Computing Studies	253	55	308	0.5
Graphic Communication	167	64	231	0.4
German	18	108	126	0.2
Business Management	35	81	116	0.2
Spanish	13	69	82	0.1
Technological studies	77	2	79	0.1
Accounting & finance	30	31	61	0.1
Information systems	48	13	61	0.1
Drama	18	41	59	0.1
Other[a]	57	111	168	0.3

Notes
Subjects ordered according to total number of qualifications gained
a 'Other' category may include more than one qualification per leaver. The 'Other' category comprises subjects with fewer than 50 course passes at SCQF level 7. These are: Religious Studies, Craft & Design, Physical Education, Classical Studies, Gaidhlig, Home Economics, Italian, Latin, Economics, Gaelic (Learners), Media Studies, Scottish Group Award, Philosophy, Psychology, Russian.

Source: Scottish Executive, 2005

Table 37: **GCE A level examination results of 16–18-year-old[a] students, by sex, subject and grade in 2003–04**

	Males			Females		
	Grade obtained (%)			Grade obtained (%)		
	A	A–E	Entries	A	A–E	Entries
Biological Sciences	20.3	93.7	17,620	24.0	95.4	26,615
Chemistry	29.6	96.1	15,841	31.1	97.3	16,289
Physics	27.3	94.6	19,223	34.2	97.2	5,383
Other Science	22.9	95.7	2,737	19.4	96.4	1,036
Mathematics	39.4	96.0	32,078	40.9	97.2	19,050
Psychology	11.3	93.5	10,786	20.6	96.5	32,021
Computer Studies	13.5	92.8	6,157	17.7	94.1	696
ICT	5.9	92.7	9,418	8.4	95.4	5,031
Design and Technology	12.3	95.6	9,504	19.7	97.9	5,978
Home Economics	–	90.2	41	16.3	97.2	498
Business Studies	13.6	97.4	18,623	16.3	98.2	12,664
Geography	20.3	98.0	16,471	29.1	98.8	13,435
History	22.2	97.9	19,065	25.1	98.5	19,085
Economics	31.1	98.0	9,512	37.1	98.5	3,896
Social Studies	18.3	95.6	16,463	21.5	96.9	28,570
Physical Education	8.3	95.5	11,360	19.5	97.1	7,874
Accounting/Finance	10.6	90.1	1,660	14.7	89.7	1,000
Art and Design	22.0	95.4	10,940	29.3	97.5	23,625
English	19.6	98.3	26,315	19.6	98.8	60,607
Communication Studies	13.5	97.9	3,095	14.7	99.0	5,214
Media/Film/TV Studies	10.0	97.9	9,066	14.9	98.7	11,924
French	34.5	98.3	4,075	32.9	98.7	8,405
German	34.6	97.2	2,021	30.6	98.3	3,622
Spanish	39.6	98.4	1,411	33.5	98.4	3,239
Other Modern Languages	40.4	95.9	1,815	47.6	97.5	2,464
Classical Studies	34.9	98.8	2,201	35.8	99.1	3,060
Music	17.1	94.8	4,248	23.5	97.7	3,982
Religious Studies	25.9	98.1	3,499	25.5	98.6	8,226
General Studies	11.5	91.7	27,009	12.8	93.7	30,181
Total	21.0	95.8	312,254	23.4	97.3	363,673

a Age at the start of the 2003/04 academic year i.e. 31 August 2003.
   Percentages based on fewer than six students are suppressed.

Source: DfES, 2004d

Section 4
Participation in post-compulsory education and training:
rates and patterns

4.1 Post-16 participation rates

In 2003, Wales had the highest staying-on rate after the end of compulsory schooling (74 per cent) and Scotland the lowest (52 per cent).

The proportion of pupils continuing their education after compulsory education in England was 72 per cent and in Northern Ireland, 70 per cent (DfES, 2004a).

The NIACE 2005 participation survey found that only about one in five adults age 17+ in the UK was currently learning (19 per cent), with 42 per cent having participated in some learning activity during the previous three years – an increase since 2004 but a decline since 2001.

Thirty-five per cent of respondents said that they had not participated in learning since leaving full-time education, a figure which has remained relatively constant for a decade (Figure 41).

The DFES National Adult Learning Survey 2002 and English Local Labour Force Surveys (ELLFS) have produced higher participation figures than the NIACE surveys. They suggest that about 77 per cent of adults in 2002–03 were involved in some type of learning and 60 per cent in taught learning.

The 2004–05 Labour Force Survey found that 69.5 per cent of adults aged 16–69 in England were engaged in some kind of learning, and 48.6 per cent in taught learning, considerably more than in the NIACE survey. The discrepancy between the NIACE and other findings is attributed to the fact

Figure 41: **Current or recent adult participation in learning, United Kingdom, 2000–05[a]**

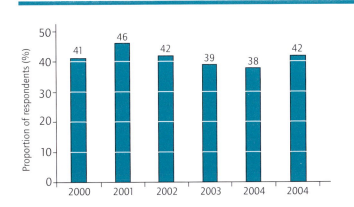

a The NIACE survey, undertaken by RSGB, interviews a weighted sample of approximately 5,000 adults, aged 17 and over, in the UK in February and March each year.

Source: Aldridge and Tuckett, 2005

that government surveys cover shorter episodes of learning than are captured in the NIACE survey (Aldridge and Tuckett, 2005).

4.2 Regional variations

In the 2005 NIACE survey, the number of current learners was higher in Wales (22 per cent) and England (20 per cent) than in Scotland (14 per cent) England and Wales also reported the highest proportion of current and recent learners (42 per cent), compared with 36 per cent in Scotland and 37 per cent in Northern Ireland (Table 38).

The NIACE survey found some variation between English regions (though lower than in previous years), with the highest rates of learning participation reported in the South West (47 per cent) and the lowest (36 per cent) in the West Midlands (Table 39).

Again, the Labour Force Survey figures are higher. The annual Local Area Labour Force Survey for 2003–04[1] found that in England, participation in learning in unitary authorities and local authority districts was about 75.8 per cent. The areas with the highest proportions were City of London (but based on too small a sample), St Albans (90.9 per cent) and Guildford (88.5 per cent). The areas with the lowest proportions were St Edmundsbury (52.6 per cent), Corby (52.9 per cent) and Easington (59.0 per cent).

In Wales the overall proportion was 66.2 per cent, with the highest proportion in Powys (73.6 per cent) and the lowest in Blaenau Gwent (50.1 per cent).

Table 38: **Adult participation in learning, by nation, United Kingdom, 2005[a]**

	Total	England	Wales	Scotland	N.Ireland
			(%)		
Current learning	19	20	22	14	17
Recent learning (in the last three years)	22	22	20	22	21
All current/recent learning	42	42	42	36	37
Past learning (more than three years ago)	24	24	21	29	15
None since leaving full-time education/ don't know	33	34	36	36	47
Weighted base	5,043	4,130	293	480	150

a The NIACE survey, undertaken by RSGB, interviewed a weighted sample of 5,053 adults, aged 17 and over, in the UK in the period 16 February–6 March 2005.
b It is necessary to remember the smaller sizes involved when examining data concerning Wales, Scotland and Northern Ireland, which should be interpreted with care.

Source: Aldridge and Tuckett, 2005

Table 39: **Adult current or recent participation in learning, by region and nation, United Kingdom, 2005[a]**

	Current or recent participation
	(%)
Total United Kingdom	42
South West	47
East of England	46
East Midlands	44
London	44
North West	44
South East	41
Yorkshire & Humber	41
North East	38
West Midlands	36
England	42
Wales	42
Northern Ireland	37
Scotland	36

a The NIACE survey, undertaken by RSGB, interviewed a weighted sample of 5,053 adults, aged 17 and over, in the UK in the period 16 February–6 March 2005.

Source: Aldridge and Tuckett, 2005

The proportion for Scotland was 66.2 per cent with the highest proportion in Midlothian (77.0 per cent) and the lowest in North Lanarkshire (52.1 per cent). The annual Local Area Labour Force Survey for 2004–05 (Table 40) nevertheless produced similar regional differences to those found in the NIACE survey with the West Midlands having the lowest proportion of adults learning and the South West having the highest, together with the south east and London which did not do so well in the NIACE survey. Again, the overall numbers of learners are somewhat higher than those found in the NIACE survey.

Table 40: **Adult participation in any learning and taught learning, England, 2004–05**

	Aged 16–69 and participating in any learning	Aged 16-69 and participating in taught learning
	(%)	(%)
England	69.5	48.6
North East	65.4	47.3
North West	67.6	46.2
Yorkshire & Humber	66.8	47.0
East Midlands	66.6	46.3
West Midlands	64.1	44.9
East	68.4	48.4
London	71.0	50.1
South East	76.1	53.0
South West	73.2	50.3

Source: *Local Labour Force Survey, 2004–05*

Table 41: **LSC-funded learners, by ethnic background, England, 2003–04**

	Further Education	Work-based Learning	Adult and community learning	6th Form	Total	Total
	(Thousands)					(%)
Asian or Asian British						
Bangladeshi	31.3	3.2	3.9	3.1	41.5	0.7
Indian	90.4	3.8	14.7	14.7	123.6	2.1
Pakistani	86.6	6.3	10.7	10.0	113.6	1.9
Any other Asian background	47.0	1.3	5.9	3.5	57.7	1.0
Black or black British						
African	108.5	3.2	8.1	6.0	125.8	2.2
Caribbean	70.8	6.5	9.2	3.9	90.4	1.5
Any other black background	21.2	2.3	2.9	1.2	27.6	0.5
Chinese	22.9	0.4	3.6	2.6	29.5	0.5
Mixed						
White and Asian	10.9	0.8	1.4	1.7	14.8	0.3
White and black African	11.5	0.8	1.0	0.6	13.9	0.2
White and black Caribbean	18.1	3.2	1.6	1.6	24.5	0.4
Any other mixed background	14.5	1.7	2.2	2.7	21.1	0.4
White						
British	3,096.5	482.2	657.8	267.9	4,504.4	77.2
Irish	31.4	1.5	6.8	1.7	41.4	0.7
Any other white background	137.0	4.2	25.1	9.0	175.3	3.0
Any other	88.0	3.0	10.9	3.7	105.6	1.8
Not known/not provided	227.6	6.4	76.4	16.7	327.1	5.6
Total	**4,114.2**	**530.9**	**842.1**	**350.6**	**5,837.8**	**100.0**

Source: LSC, 2004d

4.3 Participation in relation to ethnic background

The number of ethnic minority respondents in the NIACE 2005 survey was too small to allow for meaningful analysis. Some figures for England are available from the Learning and Skills Council (LSC) though only for LSC-funded provision. These indicate that in 2003–04, 77 per cent of learners in LSC-funded provision were white British. The highest proportions of learners from other non-white ethnic groups were Asian or Asian British Indian and black or black British African (over 2 per cent each) (Table 41).

4.4. Participation in relation to age

The NIACE 2005 survey produced the very familiar finding that learning declines with age, particularly after age 54. Only 35 per cent of adults aged 55–64, 17 per cent of adults aged 65–74 and 10 per cent of those aged 75 and over claimed to have engaged in current or recent learning, compared to 63 per cent of those aged 20–24, 52 per cent of those aged 25–34 and 49 per cent of those aged 35–44 (Table 42).

Over one-half of respondents aged 65 and over said that they had not participated in any learning since leaving full-time education.

The survey also shows a drop in the number of young adult learners (17–24) since 2002 (Table 43).

Table 43: **Current or recent adult participation in learning, by age, United Kingdom, 1996–2005[a]**

	1996		1999		2002		2005	
				(%)				
Total sample	40	(5)[b]	40	(4)	42	(4)	42	(5)
17–19	86	(42)	81	(37)	78	(34)	75	(47)
20–24	65	(15)	70	(25)	72	(27)	63	(25)
25–34	48	(2)	50	(2)	51	(2)	52	(2)
35–44	43	(1)	47	(1)	47	(2)	49	(1)
45–54	36	(1)	41	(*)	44	(1)	47	(*)
55–64	25	(*)	29	(−)	30	(−)	32	(−)
65–74	19	(2)	16	(−)	20	(−)	17	(−)
75+	15	(−)	9	(−)	10	(−)	10	(−)

a The NIACE survey, undertaken by RSGB, interviews a weighted sample of approximately 5,000 adults, aged 17 and over, in the UK in February and March each year.
b Figures in parentheses show the proportion of each age group in full-time education; * represents 0–0.5%

Source: Aldridge and Tuckett, 2005

Table 42: **Adult participation in learning, by age, United Kingdom, 2005[a]**

	Total	17–19	20–24	25–34	35–44	45–54	55–64	65–74	75+
					(%)				
Current learning	19	55	36	23	20	21	14	7	3
Recent learning (in the last three years)	22	20	26	29	29	26	19	10	7
All current/recent learning	42	75	63	52	49	47	32	17	10
Past learning (more than three years ago)	24	6	13	19	23	24	30	32	30
None since leaving full-time education/don't know	35	20	25	29	28	29	38	51	60
Weighted base	5,023	243	358	831	977	819	794	596	434

a The NIACE survey, undertaken by RSGB, interviewed a weighted sample of 5,053 adults, aged 17 and over, in the UK in the period 16 February–6 March 2005.

Source: Aldridge and Tuckett, 2005

4.5 Participation in relation to sex

The NIACE 2005 survey showed an increase in both male and female participation rates over the previous 12 months. It found that slightly more women (43 per cent) than men (40 per cent) had participated in learning during the past three years.

Comparisons with earlier survey findings indicate that since 1996, women's participation in learning has increased by five percentage points, while among men it has fallen by three points. Women (36 per cent) were, however, more likely than men (33 per cent) to say that they had not participated in any learning since leaving full-time education (Figure 42 and Table 44).

Table 44: **Adult participation in learning, men and women compared, United Kingdom, 2005[a]**

	Total	Men	Women
		(%)	
Current learning	19	19	20
Recent learning (in the last three years)	22	22	22
All current or recent learning	42	40	43
Past learning (more than three years ago)	24	27	21
None since leaving full-time education/don't know	35	33	36
Weighted base	5,053	2,444	2,609

a The NIACE survey, undertaken by RSGB, interviewed a weighted sample of 5,053 adults, aged 17 and over, in the UK in the period 16 February–6 March 2005.

Source: Aldridge and Tuckett, 2005

Figure 42: **Current or recent adult participation in learning, by sex, United Kingdom, 1996–2005[a]**

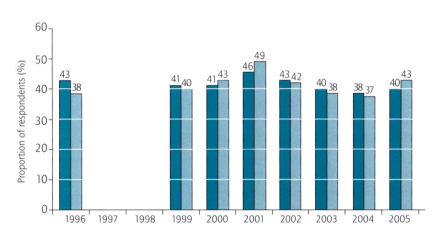

a The NIACE survey, undertaken by RSGB, interviews a weighted sample of approximately 5,000 adults, aged 17 and over, in the UK in February and March each year.

Source: Aldridge and Tuckett, 2005

A consistent feature of post-16 participation is that women are more likely to engage in organised forms of learning than men. Women are more likely than men to be learning in education and training institutions in their own time and they are also more likely than men to have workplace opportunities to learn at work. LSC figures for LSC-funded provision show that women of all ethnic backgrounds predominate in all forms of post compulsory education provision except work-based learning (Table 45).

4.6 Participation in relation to terminal age of education

The NIACE 2005 survey shows that there is a persisting gap between those who leave school at the earliest opportunity and those who stay on for even a short while.

Thirty per cent of those who left school at the earliest leaving age were current or recent learners, compared with nearly 50 per cent of those who

Table 45: **Participation in LSC-funded provision, by sex and ethnic background, England, 2003-04**

	Work-based Learning		Further Education		Adult and Community Learning	
	Female	Male	Female	Male	Female	Male
			(Thousands)			
Asian or Asian British						
Bangladeshi	1.6	1.6	16.2	15.1	3.0	0.9
Indian	1.9	1.8	54.7	35.7	11.6	3.1
Pakistani	3.6	2.7	52.3	34.3	8.9	1.8
Any other Asian background	0.5	0.8	23.6	23.4	4.6	1.3
Black or black British						
African	1.4	1.8	61.8	46.7	5.9	2.2
Caribbean	2.9	3.6	44.1	26.7	7.1	2.1
Any other black background	1.0	1.3	12.3	8.9	2.0	0.8
Chinese	0.2	0.2	14.5	8.4	2.7	0.8
Mixed						
White and Asian	0.4	0.4	5.9	5.0	1.0	0.3
White and black African	0.4	0.4	6.5	5.0	0.8	0.2
White and black Caribbean	1.6	1.7	11.0	7.1	1.3	0.4
Any other mixed background	0.9	0.9	8.9	5.6	1.6	0.5
White						
British	214.6	267.6	1,882.5	1,214.1	503.9	154.0
Irish	0.7	0.8	18.6	12.8	5.2	1.6
Any other white background	2.1	2.0	87.0	50.0	20.0	5.2
Any other	1.2	1.8	47.8	40.2	8.2	2.7
Not known/not provided	2.8	3.6	127.6	99.9	56.2	20.2
All	237.9	293.0	2,475.3	1,638.8	643.9	198.2

Source: DfES, 2005e

finished full-time education aged between 17 and 20, and 60 per cent of those who left aged 21 and over (Aldridge and Tuckett, 2005).

4.7 Participation in relation to level of qualification

Participation also remains strongly related to the level of qualifications held.

Data from Scotland indicate that in 2003, 90 per cent of those with no qualifications were not engaging in any education or training, a considerably greater number than those with some qualifications (Table 46).

The table shows relatively small levels of participation overall, with the highest being in on-the-job training. It also shows that on-the-job training increases with level of qualification (see also Section 7).

4.8 Participation in relation to socio-economic status

Socio-economic status remains a key determinant of adult participation.[2] Although the NIACE 2005 survey found that participation among all socio-economic classes has increased since 2004, particularly among C2s where it has risen from 32

Table 47: **Adult participation in learning, by socio-economic class, United Kingdom, 1996–2005[a]**

	1996	1999	2002	2005
		(%)		
Total sample	40	40	42	42
AB	53	58	60	56
C1	52	51	54	51
C2	33	36	37	40
DE	26	24	25	26
Weighted base	4,755	5,205	5,885	5,053

Base: all respondents

a The NIACE survey, undertaken by RSGB, interviews a weighted sample of approximately 5,000 adults, aged 17 and over, in the UK in February and March each year.

Source: Aldridge and Tuckett, 2005

Table 46: **Adult[a] participation in training and education, by qualifications held, Scotland, 2003**

	No qualifi-cations	'O' Grade or equivalent	Highers or equivalent	First or higher degree	Professional qualifi-cations	All
			(%)			
None	90	67	61	57	60	72
On-the-job training	6	19	23	25	28	17
Further education course	1	4	4	2	2	3
A university based course	1	5	7	9	5	4
Distance learning/university	0	2	3	4	4	2
School	0	1	1	0	0	1
Adult education or evening class	1	3	3	4	4	2
Help with reading, writing or use of numbers	0	0	0	0	0	0
Other	1	1	1	2	2	1
Base	2,152	6,693	5,422	1,474	1,572	10,038

a Aged 15–64
   Columns add to more than 100 per cent since multiple responses were allowed.

Source: Scottish Executive, 2003

to 40 per cent, there is a persisting social class divide. Around half of ABs (56 per cent) and C1s (51 per cent) participate, compared with 40 per cent of skilled manual workers (C2s) and 26 per cent of unskilled workers and people on limited incomes (DEs). Over half of DE respondents (55 per cent) have not participated in learning since leaving full-time education, compared with 17 per cent of ABs. Despite all the widening participation initiatives of recent years, participation rates among the lowest social categories – DEs – have remained broadly unchanged over time (Table 47).

The same social class patterns are reflected in government surveys. According to figures prepared by the Department for Work and Pensions for the OECD:

- Those in elementary occupations (occupations that require the knowledge and experience necessary to perform mostly routine tasks, often involving the use of simple hand-held tools and in some cases a degree of physical effort) were least likely to report learning (58 per cent).
- People in manual occupations were least likely to have undertaken some learning.
- The group with the lowest household income reported the lowest engagement in adult learning.
(OECD, 2004b)

4.9 Participation in relation to employment status

The NIACE 2005 survey found that just over half of both part-time and full-time workers were current or recent learners, compared with 40 per cent of unemployed adults (registered and claiming Job Seekers' Allowance), 30 per cent of those who were not working and 17 per cent of retired adults. Around half of those who were retired or not working said that they had not been involved in any learning since leaving full-time education, compared with one quarter of adults in employment (Aldridge and Tuckett, 2005).

Since 1996, participation in learning has increased among those in full-time employment (by 3 per cent) and part-time employment (by 11 per cent) and those who are not working (by 7 per cent), but it has remained relatively constant among the unemployed (despite an increase in 2002) and decreased by 3 per cent among retired adults (Table 48).

The increase in participation among part-time workers is important and could signify greater employer attention to their development needs than has hitherto been the case.

Table 48: **Adult participation in learning, by employment status, United Kingdom, 2005[a]**

	Total	Full-time	Part-time	Unemployed[b]	Not working	Retired
				(%)		
Current learning	19	21	25	10	14	6
Recent learning (in the last three years)	22	32	28	30	16	11
All current/recent learning	42	52	53	40	30	17
Past learning (more than three years ago)	24	22	22	21	23	32
None since leaving full-time education/don't know	35	25	25	39	47	51
Weighted base	5,053	2,002	610	227	648	1,330

a The NIACE survey, undertaken by RSGB, interviewed a weighted sample of 5,053 adults, aged 17 and over, in the UK in the period 16 February–6 March 2005.
b Unemployed includes only those who are registered as unemployed and claiming JSA.

Source: Aldridge and Tuckett, 2005

The drop since 2002 in the number of unemployed adults who are participating in learning is worrying although this could be due to the existence of other options under the New Deal programmes. The rule governing the amount of study time that JSA claimants can engage in (16 guided hours) could also be a factor.

4.10 Participation related to income

Costs could be another contributory factor. Table 49 reveals a link between benefit dependency and learning. Only 60 per cent of those on benefits reported some learning, compared with 81 per cent of the rest of the sample.

4.11 Access to the Internet

There appears to be a strong link between participation in learning and use of the Internet. In the NIACE 2005 survey, 23 per cent of those without access to the Internet reported current or recent participation in learning, compared with 56 per cent of those with Internet access. 24 per cent of those without Internet access said that they were likely to take up learning in the next three years compared with 51 per cent of those with access.

Over twice as many of those with Internet access as those without said they were likely to engage in learning in the future (Aldridge and Tuckett, 2005).

Of those adults with access to the Internet, 34 per cent had used it to find information for their learning or training and 20 per cent had used it to learn on- or off-line. Five per cent used the Internet mainly in connection with their learning.

(More information on access to and use of the Internet can be found in Section 1.17)

Table 49: **Benefit dependency groups[a] reporting adult[b] participation in different types of learning, United Kingdom, 2003**

	All	Benefit dependent	Not benefit dependent
		(%)	
Any learning	76	60	81
Taught learning	61	46	65
Self-directed learning	61	41	66
Vocational learning	69	52	73
Non-vocational learning	26	20	28
Weighted base	5,654	1,102	4,488
Unweighted base	5,725	1,129	4,528

a Respondents are classified as being benefit dependent if they report any of the following sources of household income: Jobseekers Allowance, Income Support, Invalid Care Allowance, Working Families Tax Credit and Severe Disablement Allowance.
b Base: all respondents aged 16–69

Source: *Annual Labour Force Survey*, 2003

4.12 Future intentions to learn

In the NIACE 2005 survey, 39 per cent of respondents who had left full-time education said that they were likely to take up learning in the next three years, and 57 per cent that they were unlikely to do so.[3]

As in previous years, such intentions are strongly linked with current participation. Seventy-seven per cent of current learners reported that they were likely to take up learning in the future, compared with 14 per cent of those who had not participated since leaving full-time education. Eighty-three per cent of those who had not participated in learning since leaving full-time education (reported that they had no intention of doing so in the future (Figure 43).

Future intentions to learn, by age

Reflecting participation patterns, future intentions to learn tend to decline with age (Table 50), with the steepest drop among adults aged 55 and over.

Future intentions to learn, by socio-economic status
The socio-economic profile of those declaring an intention to learn closely reflects that of current and recent participants.

Figure 43: **Future intentions to learn, by learning status, United Kingdom, 2005[a]**

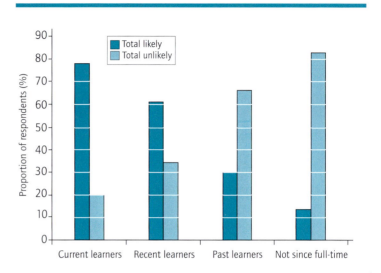

a The NIACE survey, undertaken by RSGB, interviewed a weighted sample of 5,053 adults, aged 17 and over, in the UK in the period 16 February – 6 March 2005.

Source: Aldridge and Tuckett, 2005

Table 50: **Future intentions to learn, by age, United Kingdom, 2005[a]**

	Total	17–19	20–24	25–34	35–44	45–54	55–64	65–74	75+
					(%)				
Very likely	19	28	31	29	25	22	14	6	2
Fairly likely	20	28	24	30	27	24	13	5	2
Total likely	39	56	55	58	52	45	27	11	4
Fairly unlikely	13	14	15	16	14	11	15	9	6
Very unlikely	45	23	25	23	30	39	54	77	87
Total unlikely	57	37	39	39	44	50	69	87	93
Don't know	4	7	6	3	4	5	4	2	3
Weighted base	4,816	128	268	811	969	815	794	596	434

Base: all respondents who have finished full-time education

a The NIACE survey, undertaken by RSGB, interviewed a weighted sample of 5,053 adults, aged 17 and over, in the UK in the period 16 February–6 March 2005.

Source: Aldridge and Tuckett, 2005

In the 2005 survey, one-half of respondents from classes AB and 46 per cent from class C1 said they were likely to take up learning in the future, compared with 39 per cent of C2s and 26 per cent of DEs. This situation has not changed much since 2002. Since that year, intentions to learn have increased among C2s by 3 per cent, but decreased among DEs by 2 per cent (Table 51).

Future intentions to learn, by nation and region

Again reflecting participation patterns, respondents in Wales (41 per cent) were the most likely to see themselves as future learners, while those in Scotland (37 per cent) were the least likely.

In England, those living in the East of England (44 per cent), East Midlands (43 per cent), the South East and London (42 per cent) were more likely to say they would engage in learning in the future than respondents in the rest of the country (Table 52).

4.13 Participation to gain qualifications

Government figures (DfES 2004a) indicate that in Spring 2004, 18 per cent of all people of working age in the UK were studying towards a qualification.

Unsurprisingly, those aged 16–24 were more likely to be working towards a qualification than people in other age groups. People of non-white ethnic origin were considerably more likely to be studying towards a qualification than people of white ethnic origin (28 per cent compared to 17 per cent). This confirms research indicating that people in some ethnic minority groups participate largely in order to gain qualifications that will further their employment prospects.

Table 53 shows the qualifications worked towards by different age groups.

Table 53 shows that women are more likely than men to be working towards a qualification at all ages. This reinforces the expectation expressed in

Table 51: **Future intentions to learn, by socio-economic class, United Kingdom, 2005[a]**

	Total	AB	C1	C2	DE
	(%)				
Very likely	19	26	23	19	12
Fairly likely	20	24	22	20	14
Total likely	39	50	46	39	26
Fairly unlikely	13	13	15	13	10
Very unlikely	45	35	35	44	59
Total unlikely	57	47	51	57	69
Don't know	4	2	4	4	5

Base: all respondents who have finished full-time education

a The NIACE survey, undertaken by RSGB, interviewed a weighted sample of 5,053 adults, aged 17 and over, in the UK in the period 16 February–6 March 2005.

Source: Aldridge and Tuckett, 2005

Table 52: **Future intentions to learn, by region and nation, United Kingdom, 2005[a]**

	Future intentions	
	Likely	Unlikely
	(%)	
Total United Kingdom	39	57
South West	37	58
East	44	53
East Midlands	43	54
London	42	55
North West	36	60
South East	42	54
Yorkshire & Humber	35	58
North East	36	60
West Midlands	33	63
England	39	57
Wales	41	55
Northern Ireland	40	59
Scotland	37	61

Base: all respondents who have finished full-time education

a The NIACE survey, undertaken by RSGB, interviewed a weighted sample of 5,053 adults, aged 17 and over, in the UK in the period 16 February–6 March 2005.

Source: Aldridge and Tuckett, 2005

Section 3 that women's overall qualification levels may soon outstrip those of men.

Section 5 outlines participation in different education and training sectors.

Table: 53: **Qualifications worked towards, by student profile, United Kingdom, 2004**

	Total working towards a qualification[b]		Of which, proportion working towards[c,d]				
	Number (Thousands)	Proportion	Degree or equivalent	Higher education qualification (below degree level)	GCE A-Level or equivalent	GCSE grades A*–C or equivalent	Other qualification
	(Thousands)	(%)[e]			(%)		
All people[a]	6,434	17.8	26.4	11.3	21.8	13.4	26.6
Economic activity							
Employees[f,g]	3,782	16.1	21.9	13.8	22.3	9..6	31.8
Self-employed[g,h]	192	5.8	14.9	12.7	11.7	8.9	51.8
ILO unemployed[i]	256	19.1	22.5	8.2	19.7	1.4	30.3
Economically inactive[j]	2,105	26.7	36.8	7.1	21.3	19.8	14.3
All aged							
All	6,434	17.8	26.4	11.3	21.8	13.4	26.6
16–19	2.145	70.9	12.1	5.0	46.5	26.5	9.2
20–24	1,274	35.3	57.1	12.1	9.4	4.2	16.8
25–29	628	17.8	32.6	15.9	8.9	6.4	35.4
30–39	1,138	13.0	23.9	16.5	9.6	8.5	40.9
40–49	815	9.8	20.3	15.5	9.7	8.1	46.1
50–64	434	4.8	15.1	11.3	9.7	9.3	54.1
Males aged							
All	2,933	15.8	27.6	9.8	22.8	12.8	26.5
16–19	1,070	69.4	10.9	5.0	47.6	26.2	9.6
20–24	621	34.8	58.1	10.7	10.5	3.4	16.9
25–29	297	17.2	35.8	14.2	8.5	3.8	36.9
30–39	464	10.8	26.3	15.2	6.8	5.7	45.0
40–49	305	7.5	23.0	11.8	8.5	7.2	49.3
50–64	176	3.4	17.6	9.8	6.9	7.9	57.2
Females aged							
All	3,500	19.9	25.3	12.5	21.0	14.0	26.6
16–19	1,075	72.4	13.2	4.9	45.5	26.7	8.9
20–24	653	35.7	56.1	13.3	8.3	5.0	16.7
25–29	331	18.3	29.7	17.4	9.2	8.7	34.9
30–39	674	15.9	22.3	17.5	11.6	10.4	38.9
40–49	510	12.1	18.7	17.8	10.3	8.6	44.2
50–64	258	6.8	13.3	12.4	11.6	10.3	51.9
By highest qualification held[d]							
Degree or equivalent	1,004	16.2	40.7	16.8	3.7	2.8	35.7
Higher Education qualification (below degree level)	546	17.5	36.8	23.8	5.6	3.1	30.5
GCE A-Level or equivalent	1,975	22.8	45.6	12.1	19.8	3.4	18.9
GCSE grades A*–C or equivalent	1,565	20.1	4.6	6.6	48.4	13.1	26.8
Other qualifications	695	14.4	13.8	9.4	20.3	16.5	38.7
No qualification	621	11.5	1.9	2.5	6.5	69.3	18.8

Table 53 continues on facing page

Table: 53: **continued**

	Total working towards a qualification[b]		Of which, proportion working towards[c,d]				
	Number (Thousands)	Proportion	Degree or equivalent	Higher education qualification (below degree level)	GCE A-Level or equivalent	GCSE grades A*–C or equivalent	Other qualification
	(Thousands)	(%)[e]			(%)		
By ethnic origin							
White	5,552	16.8	25.0	11.2	22.4	13.6	27.3
Non-white	878	27.7	35.1	11.8	17.7	12.2	22.1
Mixed	93	35.7	33.0	–	25.0	17.1	19.6
Asian or Asian British	390	25.1	37.2	11.5	18.6	12.9	18.8
Black or black British	236	29.9	26.8	13.6	19.6	12.9	26.0
Chinese	63	40.7	61.3	–	–	–	15.9
Other ethnic group	96	23.3	32.3	15.9	–	–	32.3
Employees							
Full-time & part-time							
All	3,782	16.1	21.9	13.8	22.3	9.6	31.8
Males	1,656	13.7	22.2	12.6	23.4	7.9	33.4
Females	2.125	18.7	21.6	14.8	21.6	11.0	30.6
Full-time							
All	2,182	12.4	19.2	16.4	15.3	7.3	41.8
Males	1,144	10.4	18.7	14.5	16.3	6.4	43.6
Females	1,039	15.8	19.5	18.3	14.1	8.1	39.4
Part-time							
All	1,598	27.2	25.9	10.5	32.2	12.8	18.5
Males	512	46.9	30.2	8.4	39.3	11.0	10.6
Females	1,086	22.7	23.7	11.4	28.7	13.7	22.1

a Only those of working age: males aged 16–64 and females aged 16–59. These figures include unpaid family workers, those on government employment and training programmes, or those who did not answer.

b For those who are working towards more than one qualification, the highest is recorded.

c Expressed as a percentage of those in the group working towards a qualification.

d Apart from rounding, figures may not sum to grand totals because of questions in the LFS which were unanswered or did not apply.

e Expressed as a percentage of the total number of people in the group

f Employees are those in employment excluding the self-employed, unpaid family workers and those on government employment or training programmes.

g The split into employee and self-employed is based on respondents' own assessment of their employment status.

h Self-employed are those in employment excluding employees, unpaid family workers and those on government employment or training programmes.

i Unemployed according to the International Labour Organization (ILO) definition.

j People who are neither in employment nor ILO unemployed.

Source: DfES, 2004b

Section 5
Education sectors and provision

In November 2005 in the UK, there were 566 institutions awarding degrees (including Foundation Degrees) directly or on behalf of 'recognised bodies' (usually universities); there were nearly 500 further education institutes (including sixth-form colleges) (Table 54).

5.1 Higher Education (HE)

Statistics below have been taken largely from the Higher Education Statistics Agency press releases and (especially) HESA, 2005, Students in Higher Education Institutions 2003/04: Reference volume.

Participation
In the 2003–04 academic year:
- The number of students following an HE programme leading to a qualification or credit at a publicly funded UK higher education institution (HEI) was 2,247,440 (2,175,115 in 2002–03).[4]
- 76.7 per cent were studying for an undergraduate qualification (at or below first degree level) and the rest for a qualification at postgraduate level.
- The number of first-year students exceeded a million for the first time. There were 3.6 per cent more first-year students than in 2002–03.
- 94.8 per cent of full-time first-degree students domiciled in England were studying in their country of domicile. The corresponding figure for Wales was 58.9 per cent, for Scotland, 93.5 per cent, and for Northern Ireland, 70.9 per cent).
- While 13,290 Scottish students entered an HE institution in the rest of the UK, the number of students coming the other way was nearly twice as high – 26,305. (While top-up fees of up to £3,000 a year are to be introduced in England

Table 54: **Number of establishments of further and higher education, United Kingdom, 2005**

Academic year 2005–06

Universities (including Open University) and other degree-awarding institutions[a,b]	114
Other higher education institutions (awarding degrees from recognised bodies)	298
Institutions awarding Foundation Degrees only	154
Further education institutions (including sixth-form colleges)	492

a Includes former polytechnics and colleges which became universities
b Including two 'federal universities' – University of Wales, with six colleges, and University of London, with 19 colleges, schools or institutes

Sources: http://www.dfes.gov.uk/recognisedukdegrees/annex4.shtml and http://www.dfes.gov.uk/recognisedukdegrees/annex5.shtml

in 2006, Scotland, Wales and Northern Ireland have not yet decided to introduce top-up fees. Figures from the Universities and Colleges Admissions Service (UCAS) indicate that in 2005, applications from English students to Scottish institutions are up by 16 per cent and to Welsh universities by 12 per cent).

Type and level of study
In the 2003–04 academic year:
- 60.6 per cent of all students were following a full-time or sandwich programme. The rest were following a part-time programme or were writing-up.
- Full-time, first-degree students made up 45.1 per cent of the HE student population.
- Students on sandwich programmes were 7.1 per cent of all undergraduates (7.4 per cent in 2002–03).
- 5.1 per cent of all students were following a course at further education (FE) level within higher education institutions.

- Postgraduate students made up 23.3 per cent of the HE total: 21.2 per cent of these were studying for a research degree and 50.1 per cent for a taught higher degree; the rest were studying for a Postgraduate Certificate of Education (PGCE).
- First-year postgraduate student numbers increased by 5.6 per cent compared with 2002–03.
- The number of first-year students studying other undergraduate programmes (such as HNDs) fell by 3.8 per cent compared with 2002–03. (Figure 44).

Higher National Diplomas (HNDs), Higher National Certificates (HNCs) and Foundation Degrees

In 2003–04:

- The numbers of HND and HNC entrants had fallen by 19.6 (16,380) and 9.2 per cent (9,720), respectively since the previous year.

Figure 44: **All HE students, by level and mode of study, United Kingdom, 2003–04**

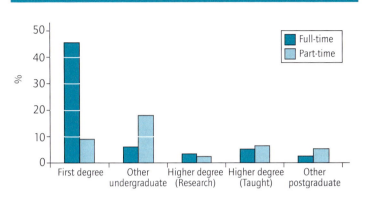

Source: HESA, 2005a

Table 55: **Number of first-year students studying for Foundation Degrees , HNDs and HNCs, by subject area, United Kingdom, 2002–03 and 2003–04**

	2003–04			2002–03		
	Foundation Degree	HND	HNC	Foundation Degree	HND	HNC
Subjects allied to medicine	1,085	265	365	665	230	160
Biological sciences	375	620	200	145	755	155
Veterinary science	0	20	0	0	40	30
Agriculture & related subjects	555	810	340	240	1,055	325
Physical sciences	100	130	135	90	195	170
Mathematical sciences	55	20	0	45	30	0
Computer science	1,050	3,365	1,310	780	4,800	1,670
Engineering & technology	1,015	2,070	2,430	655	2,365	2,755
Architecture, building & planning	125	830	1,480	145	715	1,575
Social studies	1,350	370	595	1,210	570	580
Law	35	145	40	15	115	75
Business & administrative studies	1,640	4,545	2,185	1,025	5,635	2,345
Mass communications & documentation	255	470	40	140	460	160
Languages	0	5	10	0	20	0
Historical & philosophical studies	55	5	20	0	10	0
Creative arts & design	1,290	2,305	415	875	2745	570
Education	4,425	395	160	1,750	645	140
Combined	0	5	0	515	0	0
Total	13,405	16,380	9,720	8,295	20,380	10,705

Source: HESA, 2005b

- 84.6 per cent of HND students study full time compared to 11.0 per cent of HNC students.
- The number of Foundation Degree entrants increased by 61.6 per cent.
- 21,015 students were studying on Foundation Degree programmes at UK HEIs. (This does not include students studying Foundation Degrees at further education colleges.)
- 49.3 per cent of Foundation Degree students were studying full time and 50.7 per cent part time.

Table 55 shows the number of first-year students studying for Foundation degrees, HNDs and HNCs in different subject areas in 2002–03 and 2003–04. It shows the popularity of education, business & administrative studies, computer science, engineering & technology among those studying in higher education at sub-degree level.

Part-time students

The number of part-time students has grown by 75 per cent since 1994–95. Between 2002–03 and 2003–04, there was a 2.6 per cent growth in the overall part-time UK-domiciled student body (812,475 in 2003–04, 791,625 in 2002–03). The number of part-time first-year students rose by 4.2 per cent (406,550 compared with 390,095 in 2002–03).

Part-time students now make up more than half the student body in 11 universities. Apart from Birkbeck and the Open University these are new (post-1992) universities.

In 2003–04:
- Part-time students made up 41.7 per cent of all higher education students.
- 62.4 per cent (507,345) of part-time students were women (61.6 per cent in 2002–03).
- 71.1 per cent of all part-time students were aged 30 and over (569,095).
- Nearly half of all part-time students are 'other undergraduates' (students on programmes such as Foundation Degrees, Higher National Diplomas and Higher National Certificates (HNDs and HNCs).
- The proportion of part-time students studying at

first-degree level rose by 10 per cent from 13.1 per cent in 2002–03 to 23.2 per cent.
- The proportion of part-time postgraduate students has remained static at 31.2 per cent (253,635).[5]
- 73.2 per cent of part-time students were attending an HE institution. Almost all other part-time students (26.7 per cent) were involved in UK-based distance learning. (74.1 per cent and 25.8 per cent respectively in 2002–03).

Despite their growing numbers, part-time HE students have been neglected in policy and were notably absent from consideration in the Higher Education Act. Unlike full-time students they are also discriminated against as they continue to pay fees upfront and are not entitled to the bursaries and some of the other supports that are available to full-time students. The introduction of top-up fees in 2006 could have a negative impact on part-time enrolments and this could affect the institutions such as the Open University and Birkbeck that depend on part-time students.

Part-time students by subject area

Table 56 shows that the proportion of part-time students varies greatly by subject area. In 2003–04:

- Over 90 per cent of students in the 'Combined' subject area were part-time. This is mainly attributable to the way OU students are reported.
- Other subject areas with a high proportion of part-time students were education (63.5 per cent), subjects allied to medicine (just under 50 per cent), historical and philosophical studies (44 per cent).
- Women were the majority of part-time students in most subjects, the exceptions being the physical sciences, mathematical sciences, computer science, engineering & technology, architecture, building & planning, geography and environmental sciences, economics and politics.

Motivations of part-time students

In a survey of part-time leavers in 2002–03 (response rate 70.8 per cent):

- 55.3 per cent of respondents said that they thought participation in HE would help them to get on in their current career or job.
- 23.2 per cent said they took the course because of their interest in the subject matter.
- 13.6 per cent said they took the course to help them change career or job.
- 7.9 per cent gave 'other' reasons.
  (HESA, 2004b)

In other words, nearly 70 per cent gave job-related reasons for doing the HE course.

Over 90 per cent of those who answered the question on employment were employed during or immediately before their course.

Twenty-five per cent of employed part-time students said that they did not receive any support from their employer, 19.7 per cent said that their tuition fees were paid for them, and 13.6 per cent (2,515) had their tuition fees paid and were given study leave. (HESA, 2004b).

Table 56: **Students, by subject area,[a] mode of study, sex and non-UK domicile, United Kingdom, 2003–04**

	Part-time	Female	Non-UK
		(%)	
Medicine & dentistry	20.5	56.9	13.4
Subjects allied to medicine	49.5	83.1	5.6
Biological sciences	24.9	63.8	8.5
Veterinary science	8.1	70.2	11.9
Agriculture & related subjects	23.6	59.3	13.4
Physical sciences	19.0	40.2	12.0
Mathematical sciences	25.8	38.4	15.3
Computer science	30.9	23.9	16.3
Engineering & technology	28.6	15.4	28.2
Architecture, building & planning	41.1	30.1	16.3
Social studies	37.9	62.0	14.3
Law	27.8	59.3	17.2
Business & administrative studies	37.8	50.1	24.0
Mass communications & documentation	17.1	59.7	13.2
Languages	37.1	68.0	14.9
Historical & philosophical studies	44.1	56.4	7.5
Creative arts & design	15.4	60.8	11.0
Education	63.5	73.8	6.7
Combined	91.3	59.7	3.3
Total All subject areas	39.4	57.0	13.4
Supplementary subject information[b]			
Psychology	32.2	79.1	6.8
Geography & environmental sciences	19.2	47.2	9.8
Economics & politics	13.7	39.4	30.9
English	27.8	71.7	13.9

Percentages are of all students and are not subject to rounding

a Analyses of subject information show Full Person Equivalents (FPE). These are derived by splitting student records between the different subjects that make up their qualification aim. Totals of FPE may differ slightly to counts of students due to rounding.

b Numbers reported under 'Supplementary subject information' are within and not additional to the overall total, but are disaggregated from it on a different pattern from the 19 subject areas.

Source: HESA, 2005a, Table F

HE students by domicile

In 2003–04:

- There were 300,055 students from countries other than the UK, representing 13.4 per cent of the entire HE student population (12.7 per cent in 2002–03).

- 227,340 of these were full-time and 72,720 were part-time.

- The full-time and sandwich non-UK students represented 16.7 per cent of the full-time HE student population.

- Students from countries outside the UK made up 15.3 per cent of first-year students (14.6 per cent in 2002–03).

- Students from outside the UK made up 48.4 per cent (46.7 per cent) of all full-time postgraduates, with 37.2 per cent coming from outside the EU.

- Students from outside the EU represented 9.4 per cent of the entire HE student population. (In 2005, applications from outside the EU rose by nearly 4 per cent.)

- There was a 1.1 per cent fall in the number of students from EU countries between 2002–03 and 2003–04. (In 2005, however, applications from the 10 countries that joined the EU last year rose by nearly 63 per cent.)

- There were 7,300 students from the then accession countries (the countries that acceded on 1 May 2004 were not part of the EU at the time of collection of data) – a growth of 8.2 per cent on the previous year. The majority were from Cyprus (4,210) and Poland (965). (Table 57)

Since 2003–04 there has been a decline in the number of non-UK domiciled students. Whereas there was a 9 per cent increase in overseas students in 2003–04, a survey of 70 HEIs in 2005 found that one in three universities has since experienced a drop in overseas enrolments. Applications from outside the European Union have fallen by 5.3 per cent since 2003–04; applications from China by 25.8 per cent and from Hong Kong by 6.3 per cent. The drop is largely attributed to the increase in visa fees (Baty, 2005).

Table 57a: **Non-EU European students, by country of domicile, United Kingdom, 2003–04**

	Number	Change 2002–03 to 2003–04
		(%)
Norway	3,655	−0.1
Turkey	1,960	11.7
Russia	1,880	7.4
Switzerland	1,465	11.0
Romania	615	15.0
Bulgaria	555	6.7
Ukraine	510	5.2
Yugoslavia	350	−5.4
Iceland	315	8.6
Croatia	225	40.6
Albania	190	2.7
Liechtenstein	15	0.0

Table 57b: **Non-EU European students, by country of domicile outside Europe (top 10), United Kingdom, 2003–04**

	Number
China (People's Republic of)	47,740
India	14,625
United States	13,380
Malaysia	11,805
Hong Kong	10,575
Japan	6,395
Nigeria	5,940
Taiwan	5,710
Pakistan	4,380
Singapore	3,905

Source: HESA, 2005a

HE students by age

In 2003–04:

- 54.3 per cent of first-year undergraduates of known age were aged 21 or over.
- 22.5 per cent of UK-domiciled entrants on full-time first-degree courses, and 55.9 per cent on full-time other undergraduate courses, were aged 21 and over.
- 91.4 per cent of UK domiciled entrants on part-time first-degree courses and 94.3 per cent of those on part-time other undergraduate courses, were over 21.
- 60.4 per cent of part-time first-degree entrants and 70.3 per cent of those on part-time other undergraduate courses were aged 30 or over.
- (Not shown in the table) 71.6 per cent of HNC students were over 21 while 62.4 per cent of HND students were aged 20 and under.
- 72.8 per cent of first-year Foundation Degree students were aged 21 or over
- The majority of postgraduate students were mature students. The largest proportions of postgraduates studying full-time were aged 21–24 and the largest proportion studying part-time were aged over 30.
  (Table 58)

HE students by sex

In 2003–04:

- Women made up 57 per cent of the entire HE student population (56.6 per cent in 2002–03). and 59 per cent of UK-domiciled undergraduates (58.6 per cent on 2002–03). (In 2005, 55 per cent of HE applications were from women.)
- Women were the majority among both full-time (54.4 per cent) and part-time (61.2 per cent) students.
- First-year female students (58.8 per cent) considerably outnumbered males (41.2 per cent).
- 47 per cent of students from outside the UK were women.
- The proportion of women in 'other undergraduate' programmes was 66.7 per cent.
- Nursing and other subjects allied to medicine which lead to a qualification below first-degree level attract a large majority of women students.

Table 58a: **Age distribution[a] of first-year UK-domiciled undergraduates, by mode of study, United Kingdom, 2003–04**

	First degree			Other undergraduate		
	Total	Full-time	Part-time	Total	Full-time	Part-time
	(%)			(%)		
18 and under	40.7	48.1	1.5	6.1	21.6	2.6
19 years	18.8	22.0	1.8	3.8	14.4	1.4
20 years	6.6	7.4	2.6	2.8	8.1	1.6
21–24	11.8	11.0	16.2	11.7	17.7	10.4
25–29	6.3	4.1	17.5	13.1	10.7	13.6
30 and over	15.8	7.4	60.4	62.5	27.5	70.3

Table 58b: **Age distribution[a] of first-year UK-domiciled postgraduates, by mode of study, United Kingdom, 2003–04**

	Total	Full-time	Part-time
20 and under	0.3	0.4	0.2
21–24	30.7	55.9	11.4
25–29	19.2	19.6	18.8
30 and over	49.8	24.2	69.6

Percentages are not subject to rounding
a Figures only include those students whose age is known

Source: HESA, 2005a, Tables Ii and Iii

- 65.7 per cent of first-year Foundation Degree students were women (64.1 per cent in 2002–03). Of these, 81.7 per cent were mature students (80.8 per cent in 2002–03).
- Women made up just under 53 per cent of the entire postgraduate population, and 56.4 per cent of UK domiciled postgraduates.

Table 59 shows all HE students in 2003–04 by sex, mode and domicile.

Table 59: **All HE students, by sex, mode of study and domicile, United Kingdom, 2003–04**

	UK	Other EU countries	European Union accession countries	Other EEA countries	Other Europe	Africa	Asia	Austral-asia	Middle East	North America	South America	Non EU unknown	Non-UK sub-total	Total
Full-time	1,134,905	65,010	4,965	3,395	5,930	20,020	99,545	1,325	8,760	14,830	2,765	785	227,340	1,362,245
Female	632,305	32,060	2,505	1,900	3,135	8,225	47,055	650	2,615	8,330	1,315	360	108,155	740,460
Male	502,600	32,950	2,460	1,490	2,795	11,795	52,490	675	6,145	6,505	1,450	430	119,185	621,785
Part-time	812,475	24,530	2,335	590	2,430	6,655	22,160	895	4,155	7,345	1,250	370	72,720	885,195
Female	507,345	11,990	1,290	280	1,195	2,425	10,070	445	1,665	4,040	610	200	34,210	541,555
Male	305,135	12,540	1,045	310	1,235	4,230	12,090	445	2,490	3,305	640	170	38,505	343,640
All Students	1,947,385	89,545	7,300	3,985	8,360	26,680	121,705	2,220	12,920	22,175	4,015	1,155	300,055	2,247,440
Female	1,139,650	44,050	3,800	2,180	4,330	10,650	57,125	1,095	4,280	12,365	1,925	560	142,365	1,282,015
Male	807,735	45,490	3,500	1,800	4,030	16,025	64,580	1,125	8,635	9,810	2,090	600	157,690	965,425
By domicile (%)	86.6	4.0	0.3	0.2	0.4	1.2	5.4	0.1	0.6	1.0	0.2	0.1	13.4	

In this table 0, 1, 2 are rounded to 0. All other numbers are rounded up or down to the nearest 5. Percentages are not subject to rounding.

UK figures include 3,360 full-time and 2,215 part-time students from the Channel Islands and the Isle of Man.

Source: HESA, 2005a, Table C

HE students by ethnic background

Participation in HE by students from ethnic minorities has been increasing.

In 2003–04,

- 15.3 per cent of UK-domiciled undergraduates whose ethnicity was known were from ethnic minorities.
- 14.9 per cent of first-year students and 18 per cent of all full-time first degree students of known ethnicity were from ethnic minorities (Table 60).

There are some sex differences in participation and mode of study among ethnic minority students. Figure 45 shows that in virtually all groups except Black or Black British African and Asian or Asian British Bangladeshi students, the proportion of women part-time students exceeds the proportion of full-time women students.

Table 60: **Ethnic minority students as a proportion of UK-domiciled first-year students of known ethnicity, United Kingdom, 2003–04**

	(%)
Higher degrees (research)	12.7
Full-time	13.0
Part-time	12.0
Higher degrees (taught)	16.7
Full-time	21.7
Part-time	12.8
Other postgraduate	10.4
Full-time	10.9
Part-time	10.0
First degree	17.1
Full-time	18.0
Part-time	12.0
Other undergraduate	12.9
Full-time	20.0
Part-time	11.2

Percentages are not subject to rounding

Source: HESA, 2005a, Table J

Figure 45: **Female UK-domiciled undergraduates, as a proportion of known ethnic group and mode of study, United Kingdom, 2003–04**

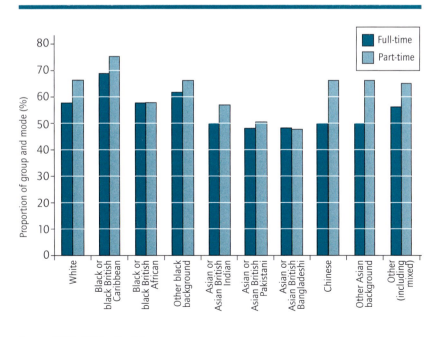

Source: HESA, 2005a, Chart 3

HE students by socio-economic background

In 2002–03:

- 87.2 per cent of young entrants to full-time first-degree courses had attended state schools (86.0 per cent in 2001–02).
- 28.4 per cent of young entrants to full-time first-degree courses came from the lowest four socio-economic groups.[6]
- 13.3 per cent of young entrants to full-time first-degree courses came from low participation neighbourhoods, an increase of 0.2 per cent on the previous year.

Research (Blanden *et al*, 2005) has revealed that educational participation in the 1990s was characterised by a narrowing in the achievement gap between rich and poor children at 16+. The study argues that the expansion of higher education since the late 1980s has disproportionately benefited those from more affluent families

HE students by disability

In 2003–04, 6.1 per cent of full-time and sandwich students who gave the information said they had a disability. Table 61 gives details.

Open University (OU) student profile

The OU student profile is different from that of conventional campus-based universities.

- The OU has a policy of open entry.
- The student population is over 210,000.
- The age-range is from 18 to 60+, with 65 per cent of students aged between 25 and 44.
- Around 75 per cent of students are working while they study, many of them in full-time employment.
- Around 60 per cent of students are studying in order to change their career or to gain promotion. (Open University website)

Table 61: **First-year UK-domiciled HE students, by qualification aim, mode of study and disability, United Kingdom, 2003–04**

	Total	Total known to have a disability	Dyslexic	Blind/ Partially sighted	Deaf/ Hearing impairment	Wheelchair user/ Mobility difficulties	Personal care support	Mental health difficulties	Autistic spectrum disorder	An unseen disability	Multiple disabilities	Other disability	No known disability	Not known / sought
Postgraduate	181,005	7,845	3,040	210	510	400	15	280	0	2,045	405	940	167,300	5,860
Full-time	78,115	4,310	1,940	110	195	190	5	140	0	1,060	140	530	71,990	1,815
Part-time	102,890	3,530	1,095	100	315	210	10	135	0	985	265	415	95,310	4,045
Undergraduate	676,495	37,700	15,660	1,065	2,100	1,655	80	1,970	80	7,110	3,405	4,575	619,865	18,930
Full-time	372,835	24,760	13,000	640	995	725	35	875	70	4,665	1,170	2,600	345,305	2,770
Part-time	303,665	12,940	2,665	420	1110	935	45	1,095	10	2,445	2,240	1,975	274,565	16,160
All levels	857,505	45,545	18,700	1,275	2,610	2,060	90	2,250	80	9,155	3,815	5,515	787,170	24,790
Full-time	450,950	29,070	14,940	750	1,190	915	40	1,015	70	5,725	1,310	3,130	417,295	4,585
Part-time	406,555	16,470	3,760	520	1,425	1,145	55	1,230	10	3,430	2,505	2,390	369,875	20,205

In this table 0, 1, 2 are rounded to 0. All other numbers are rounded up or down to the nearest 5

Source: HESA, 2005a, Table 11b

HE subject choice

In 2003–04 as in the previous year, the most popular subject group among first-degree students was business & administrative studies (12.5 per cent of students). Biological sciences and social studies were the second most popular subject groups (9.2 per cent). The subjects with the lowest number of students were mathematical sciences (1.9 per cent), agriculture and related subjects (0.6 per cent) and veterinary science (0.3 per cent) (Table 62) (see page opposite).

Variations in course choice

As usual, there are marked sex differences in subject choices.

In 2003–04:

- Subject areas with a high proportion of women students were subjects allied to medicine (83.1 per cent), education (73.8 per cent), veterinary science (70.2 per cent), and languages (68.0 per cent).
- Subject areas with a high proportion of men included engineering & technology (84.6 per cent), computer science (76.1 per cent), and architecture building & planning (69.9 per cent).
- Students from outside the UK were well represented in engineering & technology, business & administrative studies, law, mathematical sciences, languages, computer science, and architecture building & planning.
- Students on sandwich programmes formed the highest proportion in agriculture & related subjects, computer science, business & administrative studies, architecture building & planning, and engineering & technology.
- The most popular subjects among Foundation Degree students were education, social studies, business & administrative studies and creative arts & design.

Participation in science, engineering & technology

Research conducted by the University of Warwick for the Royal Society has found that men are four times more likely than women to be studying (or working in) science. Black Caribbean (especially men) and Bangladeshi people (especially women) are the

most under-represented groups in science, engineering & technology (the Royal Society, 2005) A total of 1.6 per cent of the Bangladeshi population and 2.3 per cent of the black Caribbean population are involved in science, engineering or technology, compared to just over 5.3 per cent of the white ethnic population. Asian groups are in general well represented. Chinese and Indian groups are over-represented compared to the white UK population. Black Africans are also well represented, but the black Caribbean population is under-represented

Retention rates

In 2002–03, as in previous years, a considerably higher proportion of mature full-time first-degree entrants (14.9 per cent) than young entrants (7.3 per cent) did not continue in HE following their first year.

Certain courses have particularly high non-completion rate. HESA figures for mature students on full-time first-degree courses in 2001–02 showed high rates of drop-out – over 20 per cent – particularly among those without A-levels, from the following subject areas:

- Biological and physical sciences
- Architecture, building & planning
- Business & administrative studies
- Librarianship and information studies
- Mathematical sciences and computer sciences
- Combined studies.

Foundation degrees (which attract mainly mature students) also have a high level of non-completion. 34 Foundation Degree courses reviewed by the Quality Assurance Agency found that between 45 and 90 per cent of students completed and achieved the award. On average, the withdrawal rate for full-time students is about 21 per cent and about 29 per cent for part-time students (THES, 2005).

In 2002–03, a slightly higher proportion of young full-time 'other undergraduates' (HND and foundation degree entrants) (18.7 per cent) than mature entrants (17.1 per cent) did not continue following their first year.

Table 62: **All students, by subject area, level and mode of study, United Kingdom, 2003–04**

	Higher degrees (research)			Higher degrees (taught)			Other postgraduate			First degree			Other undergraduate		
	Total	Full-time	Part-time	Total	Full-time	Part-time	Total	Full-time	Part-time	Total	Full-time	Part-time	Total	Full-time	Part-time
		(%)			(%)			(%)			(%)			(%)	
Medicine & dentistry	8.2	6.8	9.6	1.9	1.6	2.2	1.6	0.4	2.2	3.0	3.6	0.0	0.1	0.2	0.0
Subjects allied to medicine	5.7	4.9	6.5	7.5	3.1	11.0	8.4	2.4	11.2	8.6	7.0	16.9	28.4	52.8	20.3
Biological sciences	12.0	14.0	10.0	4.6	4.8	4.5	1.5	1.2	1.6	9.2	9.2	8.8	1.7	2.3	1.5
Veterinary science	0.4	0.5	0.4	0.0	0.0	0.0	0.1	0.3	0.0	0.3	0.3	0.0	0.0	0.0	0.0
Agriculture & related subjects	1.1	1.2	1.0	0.7	0.9	0.6	0.1	0.1	0.2	0.6	0.7	0.2	0.8	2.0	0.4
Physical sciences	11.0	14.5	7.4	2.6	3.3	2.0	0.5	0.5	0.5	4.1	4.6	1.7	0.8	0.5	0.9
Mathematical sciences	2.2	3.0	1.4	1.1	1.2	1.0	0.5	0.2	0.7	1.9	1.9	1.8	0.4	0.3	0.4
Computer science	4.3	4.9	3.7	6.7	8.7	5.1	1.9	1.7	2.0	7.0	7.2	6.2	5.3	6.6	4.9
Engineering & technology	13.2	15.7	10.5	7.8	9.8	6.2	2.5	1.6	2.9	6.6	6.9	5.3	3.0	4.0	2.7
Architecture, building & planning	1.8	1.8	1.7	3.0	2.5	3.3	2.6	3.4	2.2	2.3	2.1	3.2	1.4	1.4	1.4
Social studies	9.4	9.1	9.7	9.8	12.5	7.6	4.3	3.1	4.9	9.2	9.2	9.2	7.4	3.6	8.7
Law	1.9	1.9	2.0	4.3	5.4	3.4	7.0	12.8	4.4	4.7	4.6	5.4	0.6	0.7	0.6
Business & administrative studies	4.9	4.1	5.7	27.9	28.0	27.8	14.7	3.8	19.7	12.5	13.4	8.0	9.3	10.8	8.7
Mass communications & documentation	0.8	0.7	0.9	2.8	3.5	2.3	0.8	1.5	0.4	2.7	3.1	0.6	0.8	1.3	0.6
Languages	6.4	6.1	6.6	3.6	4.4	3.1	0.6	1.0	0.3	6.6	7.1	3.8	7.4	2.7	8.9
Historical & philosophical studies	7.5	6.3	8.9	3.6	2.9	4.1	0.5	0.4	0.6	5.1	4.9	6.5	4.2	0.5	5.4
Creative arts & design	2.8	2.2	3.5	4.0	5.5	2.8	1.0	2.1	0.5	8.8	10.1	2.2	3.6	6.2	2.8
Education	6.2	2.3	10.3	8.0	1.9	12.8	50.0	63.4	43.9	3.5	3.3	4.4	9.2	2.4	11.4
Combined	0.1	0.1	0.2	0.1	0.0	0.2	1.4	0.0	2.0	3.3	0.8	15.8	15.7	1.6	20.3
Supplementary subject information[a]															
Psychology	3.3	3.4	3.2	2.8	2.4	3.1	0.9	0.8	0.9	4.1	3.8	5.5	0.6	0.3	0.7
Geography & environmental sciences	2.5	2.9	2.2	1.5	1.8	1.2	0.3	0.2	0.3	2.2	2.4	1.2	0.3	0.2	0.3
Economics & politics	4.0	4.4	3.6	4.0	6.8	1.7	0.6	0.8	0.5	3.5	4.0	1.0	0.3	0.3	0.3
English	2.3	2.3	2.3	1.4	1.5	1.3	0.2	0.5	0.1	3.4	3.5	2.4	2.2	2.3	2.1

Percentages are not subject to rounding.

a Numbers reported under 'Supplementary subject information' are within and not additional to the overall total, but are disaggregated from it on a different pattern from the 19 subject areas.

Source: HESA, 2005a, Table E

Performance indicators covering the 2002–03 academic year projected an overall UK-wide 14.1 per cent drop-out rate for full-time first-degree students at UK universities and students in higher education colleges (HESA, 2004b).

HE qualifications obtained

In 2003–04,

- A total of 595,640 qualifications were awarded at HE level to students in publicly funded HEIs or on indirectly funded HE programmes in further education colleges. Of these, 30.6 per cent were at postgraduate level, 49.0 per cent were undergraduate first degrees, and 20.4 per cent were other undergraduate qualifications.
- Of those gaining a first degree in 2003–04, 11 per cent gained a first class honours degree (10 per cent in 2002–03) and 44 per cent an upper second (45 per cent in 2002–03).
- 10 per cent of first-degree graduates gained their award through part-time and other modes of study in 2003–04 (11 per cent in 2002–03).
- As in 2002–03, 56 per cent of first-degree graduates in 2003–04 were women.

- 43 per cent of first-degree graduates achieved their qualification in a science discipline. Of these, 48 per cent were women.
- 156,800 students obtained HE qualifications at postgraduate level in 2003–04. Of these, 17 per cent were awarded a Postgraduate Certificate of Education (PGCE), 9 per cent completed their studies mainly by research, and a further 74 per cent obtained qualifications after following taught postgraduate courses other than PGCE.
- The number awarded other undergraduate qualifications was 101,000 in 2003–04, an increase of 7 per cent from 2002–03.
- 38,300 undergraduate and 53,300 postgraduate students obtaining HE qualifications in 2003–04 in the UK came from overseas. Overseas students accounted for 17 per cent of all students awarded HE qualifications in 2003–04.
  (Table 63).

Table 63: **HE qualifications obtained, by level of qualification, mode of study and domicile, United Kingdom, 2003–04**

	All qualifications	Higher degree (research)	Higher degree (taught)	Other postgraduate	First degree	Other undergraduate	Of which, Foundation Degree
Full-time	425,260	13,960	65,060	39,785	260,450	46,000	2,275
UK domiciled	335,580	7,990	23,670	34,380	229,250	40,295	2,015
Non-UK domiciled	89,680	5,975	41,390	5,405	31,200	5,710	260
Part-time	170,380	4,215	27,475	31,585	31,640	75,465	860
UK domiciled	157,480	3,280	22,455	29,075	29,310	73,355	855
Non-UK domiciled	12,900	930	5,020	2,510	2,330	2,110	5
All students	595,640	18,175	92,535	71,370	292,090	121,465	3,135
Proportion of all qualifications (%)	100.0	3.1	15.5	12.0	49.0	20.4	0.5
UK domiciled	493,060	11,270	46,125	63,455	258,560	113,650	2,870
Non-UK domiciled	102,580	6,905	46,410	7,915	33,530	7,815	265

In this table 0, 1, 2 are rounded to 0. All other numbers are rounded up or down to the nearest 5. Percentages are not subject to rounding.

Source: HESA, 2005a, Table K

Degree grades

In 2003–04:

- 59.4 per cent of students were awarded a first or upper second honours degree.
- Of those gaining a first degree, 11 per cent obtained a first class honours award compared to 10 per cent in the previous year, and 44 per cent obtained an upper second class honours award (45 per cent in the previous year).

Figure 46 shows how these are distributed in relation to sex, mode and domicile. Whereas the proportion of those gaining a first-class degree did not vary greatly between different groups, the highest proportion of those gaining upper seconds were female students, full-time students and those domiciled in the UK.

Table 64 shows that there are variations by subject area in the proportions of different classes of degrees awarded. The highest number of first class degrees was awarded in maths, the sciences, and engineering & technology, and the highest number of upper seconds in historical and philosophical studies, English and languages. Among non-clinical subjects, the latter three had the highest percentages of first and second class honours degrees overall.

Destinations of full-time and part-time first degree graduates[7]

Full-time, first-degree graduates

In 2002–03, of the 182,300 full-time first-degree graduates whose destinations were known:

- 62.8 per cent (114,400) were in employment only.
- 8.0 per cent (14,500) were in a combination of work and study.
- 16.0 per cent (29,100) were involved in further study only.
- 7.1 per cent (12,900) were assumed to be unemployed.
- Of all leavers whose destinations were known in 2002–03, 7.2 per cent of males were unemployed, compared to 4.2 per cent of females.

Figure 46: **Degree classsification, by sex, domicile and mode of study, United Kingdom, 2003–04**

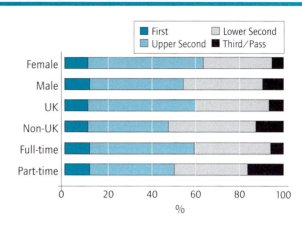

Source HESA, 2005a, Chart 4

Table 64: **First-degree graduates in non-clinical subjects awarded first or upper second class honours, United Kingdom, 2003–04**

	First class	Upper second	First or upper second
	(%)		
Subjects allied to medicine	12.4	48.9	61.3
Biological sciences	11.0	49.1	60.1
Agriculture & related subjects	10.5	44.9	55.4
Physical sciences	17.3	42.8	60.1
Mathematical sciences	26.9	34.4	61.2
Computer science	13.1	38.2	51.2
Engineering & technology	17.9	39.8	57.8
Architecture, building & planning	10.6	43.1	53.7
Social studies	8.7	51.5	60.2
Law	5.3	51.6	56.9
Business & administrative studies	6.7	42.4	49.1
Mass communications & documentation	7.3	51.6	58.9
Languages	12.3	58.6	70.9
Historical & philosophical studies	11.8	59.1	70.9
Creative arts & design	11.5	49.3	60.7
Education	8.0	45.8	53.8
Combined	11.4	43.0	54.5
Total non-clinical subjects	11.2	47.5	58.6
Supplementary subject information[a]			
Psychology	10.0	56.0	65.9
Geography & environmental sciences	9.1	51.7	60.8
Economics & politics	10.6	52.2	62.9
English	11.3	58.8	70.1

Percentages are not subject to rounding
The table excludes the clinical subject areas medicine & dentistry and veterinary science, in which the proportion of degrees awarded without classification is substantial.
a Numbers reported under 'Supplementary subject information' are within and not additional to the overall total, but are disaggregated from it on a different pattern from the 19 subject areas

Source: HESA, 2005a, Table M

Employment

About 96 per cent of those reporting employment were working in the UK:

- 26.3 per cent in Associate Professional and Technical Occupations.
- 24.6 per cent in Professional Occupations.
- 18.3 per cent in Administrative and Secretarial Occupations.
- 1.1 per cent in 'Sales and Customer Service Occupations'.
- The average salary reported (to the nearest thousand) by the 48.4 per cent who disclosed their salary, was £17,000.

Unemployment[8]

Unemployment rates for full-time first-degree graduates ranged from those in subject areas that have very low rates – medicine & dentistry (0.2 per cent); subjects allied to medicine (2.8 per cent) and Veterinary science (2.9 per cent) – to subject areas which have much higher unemployment rates: computer science (12.4 per cent); creative arts & design (10.5 per cent).

Part-time, first-degree graduates

In 2002–03, of the 20,200 part-time first-degree graduates whose destination was known:

- 65.6 per cent (13,200) were in employment only.
- 16.5 per cent (3,300) were in a combination of work and study.
- 5.9 per cent (1,200) were involved in further study only.
- 3.7 per cent (700) were assumed to be unemployed.

Of those first-degree graduates (both full-time and part-time) whose destination was known, and reported as further study (including those in a combination of work and study) in 2002–03:

- 31.7 per cent were undertaking a higher degree by taught course.
- 22.3 per cent were undertaking a postgraduate diploma or certificate.
- 15.4 per cent were undertaking a professional qualification.
- 8.4 per cent were undertaking a higher degree by research.

Destinations of other undergraduates

Of the 32,800 leavers (both full-time and part-time) who obtained undergraduate diplomas and certificates (including foundation degrees) in 2002–03, and whose destination was known:

- 53.1 per cent (17,400) were in employment only.
- 19.2 per cent (6,300) were in a combination of work and study.
- 21.6 per cent (7,100) were in further study only.
- 2.9 per cent (900) were assumed to be unemployed.

Destinations of Foundation Degree graduates

In 2002–03, of the 800 (both full-time and part-time) graduates whose destination was known:

- 30.5 per cent (200) reported their first destination as employment only.
- 23.5 per cent (200) were in a combination of work and study.
- 40.1 per cent (300) were involved in further study only.
- 4.2 per cent (35) were assumed to be unemployed.

Destinations of postgraduates

In 2002–03, of the 72,300 former postgraduate students (both full-time and part-time) whose destination was known:

- 75.6 per cent (54,600) were in employment only.
- 11.7 per cent (8,500) were in a combination of work and study.
- 6.1 per cent (4,400) were involved in further study only.
- 3.1 per cent (2,300) were assumed to be unemployed.

Destinations of students in teacher training

In 2003–04, of those leavers who had completed an Initial Teacher Training (ITT) course leading to Qualified Teacher Status (QTS) whose destinations were known, 89 per cent were currently employed in a teaching post.

Student support

In the academic year 2002–03, nearly half the total income of undergraduate students aged under 25 came from student loans, hardship loans and Access/Hardship scheme funds, and over 80 per cent of students had some income from these sources. By the end of the academic year, the majority (87 per cent) were in debt, and the average debt for all students was just under £5,500. Factors associated with having high amounts of debt were: living in rented accommodation not owned by the university and other living costs.

The introduction of top-up fees in England 2006 is expected to increase the amount of future debt among HE students.

5.2 Further education (FE)

Much of the data in this section have been drawn from evidence presented by Paul Mount, Learning and Skills Analysis Division DfES, at the NIACE FE Review inaugural meeting of the External Reference Group.

Participation in FE in the UK

Table 65 shows the students in further education in the UK by country, mode, sex and area of learning, 2002–03.

Table 65a: **Students in FE, by mode of study, sex and area of learning, United Kingdom, 2002–03: Home and overseas students**

	All		Men		Women	
	(Thousands)					
	Full-time	Part-time	Full-time	Part-time	Full-time	Part-time
Business Administration, Management & Professional	64.0	339.8	28.5	102.5	35.5	237.3
Construction	41.0	102.6	39.2	94.7	1.8	7.9
Engineering, Technology & Manufacturing	40.7	106.0	36.0	90.7	4.8	15.3
English, Languages & Communications	42.5	178.9	16.5	69.4	26.0	109.5
Foundation programmes	77.0	281.9	39.2	118.7	37.7	163.2
Hairdressing & Beauty Therapy	44.2	87.8	2.8	15.1	41.3	72.7
Health, Social Care & Public Services	154.8	487.4	63.7	154.6	91.1	332.7
Hospitality, Sports, Leisure & Travel	59.1	237.2	30.1	81.9	29.0	155.2
Humanities	66.3	83.6	24.7	24.2	41.6	59.4
Information & Communication Technology	81.6	733.2	52.8	268.2	28.7	465.0
Land-based provision	15.8	49.2	8.1	21.4	7.8	27.8
Retailing, Customer Service & Transportation	7.1	66.2	4.7	26.2	2.4	40.0
Science & Mathematics	50.6	96.8	26.5	35.8	24.2	61.1
Visual & Performing Arts & Media	80.5	155.5	35.0	45.4	45.6	110.1
Other subjects	16.1	82.0	5.8	32.3	10.3	49.7
Unknown	185.4	613.6	95.9	242.9	89.5	370.7
All subjects	1,026.7	3,701.6	509.3	1,423.9	517.5	2,277.7

Source: DfES, 2004b, Table 3.5

Table 65b: **Of which overseas students**

	All		Men		Women	
	(Thousands)					
	Full time	Part time	Full time	Part time	Full time	Part time
Business Administration, Management & Professional	0.3	0.8	0.1	0.4	0.1	0.3
Construction	–	0.1	–	0.1	–	–
Engineering, Technology & Manufacturing	0.1	1.2	0.1	1.1	–	0.1
English, Languages & Communications	0.8	2.0	0.4	0.9	0.4	1.2
Foundation programmes	–	–	–	–	–	–
Hairdressing & Beauty Therapy	0.1	0.1	–	–	0.1	0.1
Health, Social Care & Public Services	0.1	0.2	–	0.1	0.1	0.1
Hospitality, Sports, Leisure & Travel	0.1	0.1	–	–	–	0.1
Humanities	–	–	–	–	–	–
Information & Communication Technology	0.1	0.3	0.1	0.1	–	0.1
Land-based provision	0.1	0.2	–	0.1	–	0.1
Retailing, Customer Service & Transportation	–	0.3	–	0.2	–	–
Science & Mathematics	0.1	0.1	–	–	–	0.1
Visual & Performing Arts & Media	0.1	0.1	–	–	0.1	0.1
Other subjects	2.2	3.5	0.7	1.7	1.5	1.8
Unknown	10.0	25.9	5.0	11.2	5.0	14.7
All subjects	13.9	34.8	6.6	16.0	7.3	18.8
Of which European Union	4.7	8.2	1.9	3.5	2.9	4.7
Other Europe	0.6	1.8	0.2	0.5	0.4	1.3
Commonwealth	1.5	1.6	0.9	1.1	0.7	0.5
Other countries	7.0	23.2	3.7	10.9	3.4	12.3

Source: DfES, 2004b, Table 3.5

Participation in FE in England

There are 393 FE colleges in England (429 in mid-2000). They include:

- 253 General FE and Tertiary Colleges (GFEC)
- 102 Sixth Form Colleges (SFC)
- 16 Specialist Designated Colleges (SDC)
- 17 Agriculture and Horticulture colleges (AHC)
- 5 Art, Design and Performing Arts Colleges (DPAC)

Most (73 per cent) of FE college income was from the LSC; 11 per cent was from fees, paid by both employers and individuals, and 16 per cent from other sources (HEFCE and EU grants, traded services and financial income) (DfES analysis of 02/3 college accounts).

The mean average fees charged by colleges during 2003–04 were £1.85 an hour for accredited and qualification bearing provision and £2.32 an hour for non-accredited and internally accredited provision (NIACE, 2005).

Since the mid 1990s, there has been a significant expansion in learner numbers in FE in England. This has been largely due to an expansion in provision of short courses at GFECs which have attracted adults over the age of 19 as shown in Figure 47. Many of

Figure 47: **FE sector learner numbers, England, 1996–2004**

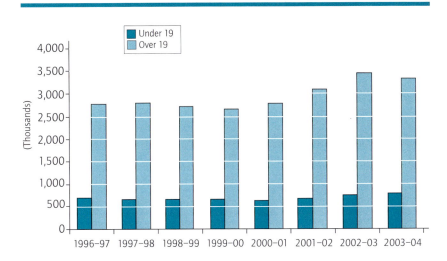

Note: Figures include external institutions.

Source: LSC, 2004d

these are part-time courses that are not accredited and qualification-bearing.

In 2003–04, over 3 million of the 4 million-plus total learners were enrolled in general further education colleges (GFECs) in England. Seventy-one per cent of these were people over 19 studying part time, mostly taking courses at Entry Level and Levels 1 and 2.

Those under 19 were considerably more likely than learners over that age to be studying full-time and in a specialist college (Tables 66 and 67).

Table 66: **Learners, by type of college, England, 2003–04**

	Under 19	Over 19	All ages
	(Thousands)		
General FE colleges	524	2,499	3.013
Sixth-form colleges	134	95	229
External institutions	38	711	749
Other colleges	5	108	113
FE sector	701	3,413	4,114
	(%)		
General FE colleges	13	61	73
Sixth-form colleges	3	2	6
External institutions	1	17	18
Other colleges	0	3	3
FE sector	17	83	100

Note: figures include external institutions, many of which are LEA-maintained providers

Source: LSC, 2004d

Table 67: **Learners, by age and mode of study, England, 2003–04**

	Full-time		Part-time		
	Under 19	Over 19	Under 19	Over 19	Total
GFEC (Thousands)	401	347	123	2,152	3,023
GFEC (% total learners)	13	11	4	71	
SFC (Thousands)	129	8	5	87	229
SFC (% total learners)	56	3	2	38	

Source: LSC, 2004d

Participation in FE in Wales

In Wales in 2002–03 there were a total of 501,450 enrolments in further education, of which 264,520 were full-time and 226,670 were part-time

Participation in LSC-funded provision

According to The Learning and Skills Council (LSC 2005b), there were an estimated 2.26 million learners in LSC-funded FE in England on 1 October 2004 – a fall of 1 per cent since 2003.

Between October 2003 and October 2004:

- The number of learners aged 19 and over in LSC provision dropped by 3 per cent to 1.63 million.
- The number of adults aged 60 and over decreased by 7 per cent.
- The total number of adults on Level 2 programmes decreased by 6 per cent.

However,

- The number of adult learners on full Level 2 programmes (5 GCSEs, an NVQ Level 2 or the equivalent) increased by 1 per cent.
- The numbers of learners on programmes contributing to the Skills for Life target increased by 19 per cent.
(Tables 68 and 69).

Table 69 gives a detailed breakdown of learners in LSC-funded provision in 2003 and 2004 by institution type, mode of attendance and age

Characteristics of learners in FE

In 2003–04 in England:

- 61 per cent of learners in FE were female, 39 per cent were male.
- 79 per cent of learners (in October 2004) were recorded as being of white ethnicity and about 17 per cent from ethnic minorities (information is not available for the remaining 4 per cent of learners). (DfES, 2005e).
- 37 per cent of learners were eligible for Widening Participation Uplift.[9]

Table 68: **Learners on LSC-funded FE provision, by level, England 2003–04**

	Under 19	19 plus	All ages
	(%)		
Level 1 and Entry	3	36	39
Level 2	4	21	25
Level 3	9	11	20
Level 4, 5 and HE	0	2	2
Level not specified	0	13	14
All levels	17	83	100

Note: Figures include external institutions

Source: LSC, 2004d

- The proportion of GFEC learners resident in a widening participation postcode was 29.3 per cent.
- 47 per cent of those eligible for the widening participation uplift were enrolled in short qualification courses compared to 41 per cent of learners not receiving the uplift.
(Source: DfES analysis of ILR data)

Table 69: **Learners on LSC-funded FE provision, by institution type, mode of attendance and age, England, 2003 and 2004**

			2003	2004 (Thousands)	% change 2003 to 2004 (%)
General FE and tertiary colleges	Full-time full year	Under 19	378.9	391.5	3.3
		19–24	71.7	73.7	2.7
		25–59	80.6	70.1	−13.1
		60 and over	2.0	1.5	−27.1
		Unknown	0.1	0.2	112.6
	Other full-time	Under 19	5.7	6.1	6.5
		19–24	7.1	6.8	−4.2
		25–59	23.0	17.8	−22.7
		60 and over	1.1	0.6	−45.1
		Unknown	–	–	–
	Part-time	Under 19	75.5	71.0	−6.0
		19–24	152.2	160.9	5.7
		25–59	836.3	815.7	−2.5
		60 and over	122.0	110.8	−9.2
		Unknown	3.2	3.4	4.4
Total			1,759.7	1,730.1	−1.7
Sixth-form colleges	Full-time full year	Under 19	129.1	137.5	6.5
		19–24	2.3	2.6	14.2
		25–59	1.3	1.1	−11.7
		60 and over	–	–	–
		Unknown	–	–	–
	Other full-time	Under 19	0.2	0.1	−64.4
		19–24	0.1	0.1	−42.6
		25–59	0.4	0.3	−37.0
		60 and over	–	–	–
		Unknown	–	–	–
	Part-time	Under 19	3.3	3.5	8.7
		19–24	5.3	4.9	−6.7
		25–59	0.4	0.3	−37.0
		60 and over	6.3	5.6	−11.2
		Unknown	0.2	0.2	−23.3
Total			183.2	186.5	1.8
Other colleges	Full-time full year	Under 19	11.4	12.4	9.0
		19–24	2.3	2.6	10.1
		25–59	2.1	2.0	−1.8
		60 and over	0.1	0.1	0.4
		Unknown	–	–	–
	Other full-time	Under 19	0.1	–	−44.8
		19–24	0.1	0.1	−19.8
		25–59	0.7	0.4	−39.6
		60 and over	–	0.1	14.2
		Unknown	–	–	–
	Part-time	Under 19	1.7	1.5	−12.3
		19–24	4.8	4.7	−2.7
		25–59	51.0	47.5	−6.8
		60 and over	29.6	29.0	−1.9
		Unknown	1.4	1.7	26.0
Total			105.3	102.2	−3.0

Table 69 continued overleaf

Table 69: **continued**

			2003	2004 (Thousands)	% change 2003 to 2004 (%)
External institutions	Full-time full year	Under 19	0.7	0.9	19.9
		19–24	0.9	0.8	−11.4
		25–59	2.6	1.8	−32.8
		60 and over	0.1	0.1	−37.0
		Unknown	–	–	–
	Other full-time	Under 19	0.1	0.1	−41.5
		19–24	0.3	0.3	−4.3
		25–59	1.6	1.6	2.5
		60 and over	0.1	0.1	−37.0
		Unknown		–	–
	Part-time	Under 19	8.3	6.9	−16.4
		19–24	17.1	18.3	7.2
		25–59	166.8	165.9	−0.5
		60 and over	40.8	39.4	−3.2
		Unknown	3.2	3.3	3.0
Total			242.8	239.6	−1.3
All institutions			2,290.9	2,268.2	−1.4

Source: LSC, 2005b

Details of FE learners by age, sex, ethnicity, highest qualification and mode of attendance are given in Tables 70 and 71.

The tables show both the preponderance of students aged over 19 and the preponderance of women students. They also show that there are considerably more ethnic minority students in FE than in work-based learning

Table 70: **Learners enrolled in LSC-funded FE provision, by age, mode of attendance and sex, England, 2003 and 2004**

		2003	2004 (provisional)	Change
		(Thousands)		(%)
By age	Below 19	615.0	631.5	2.7
	19–59	1,465.6	1,430.7	−2.4
	60 and over	202.1	187.2	−7.4
	Age unknown	8.2	8.8	7.6
By mode of attendance	Full-time full-year	686.4	698.9	1.8
	Other full-time	40.8	34.4	−15.7
	Part-time	1,563.7	1,524.9	−2.5
By sex	Female	1,404.3	1,387.5	−1.2
	Male	886.6	870.7	−1.8
All learners at 1 October		2,290.9	2,258.2	−1.4

Source: LSC, 2005b

Table 71: **Learners on LSC-funded work-based learning and FE provision, by ethnicity and sex, England, 2003 and 2004**

Work-based learning

| Ethnicity | 2003 | | | | 2004 | | | | |
	Female	Male	All	% of total	Female	Male	All	% of total	% change 2003–2004
	(Thousands)				(Thousands)				
Asian or Asian British									
Bangladeshi	0.8	0.7	1.5	0.5	0.8	0.8	1.6	0.5	6.7
Indian	1.1	1.0	2.1	0.7	1.0	1.1	2.1	0.6	0.0
Pakistani	1.9	1.3	3.2	1.0	1.8	1.3	3.1	1.0	−3.1
Any other Asian background	0.3	0.4	0.7	0.2	0.3	0.5	0.7	0.2	0.0
Black or black British									
African	0.6	0.8	1.4	0.5	0.7	0.9	1.6	0.5	14.3
Caribbean	1.3	1.8	3.1	1.0	1.5	1.9	3.4	1.1	9.7
Any other black background	0.5	0.7	1.3	0.4	0.5	0.7	1.2	0.4	−7.7
Chinese	0.1	0.1	0.2	0.1	0.1	0.1	0.2	0.1	0.0
Mixed									
White and Asian	0.2	0.2	0.4	0.1	0.2	0.3	0.5	0.2	25.0
White and black African	0.2	0.2	0.4	0.1	0.2	0.2	0.4	0.1	0.0
White and black Caribbean	0.7	0.7	1.4	0.5	0.9	1.0	1.9	0.6	0.0
Any other mixed background	0.4	0.4	0.8	0.3	0.5	0.5	1.0	0.3	0.0
White									
British	117.4	167.6	285.0	91.9	118.9	175.1	294.0	92.0	3.2
Irish	0.4	0.4	0.8	0.3	0.3	0.5	0.8	0.3	0.0
Any other white background	1.0	1.0	2.0	0.6	1.2	1.2	2.4	0.7	20.0
Any other	0.7	1.1	1.8	0.6	0.7	1.0	1.6	0.5	−11.1
Not known/not provided	1.8	2.5	4.3	1.4	1.2	1.9	3.1	1.0	−27.9
Total	**129.4**	**180.9**	**310.4**	**100.0**	**130.8**	**188.9**	**319.7**	**100.0**	**3.0**

Table 71 continues overleaf

Table 71: **continued**

Further education

Ethnicity	2003				2004				% change 2003–2004
	Female	Male	All	% of total	Female	Male	All	% of total	
	(Thousands)				(Thousands)				
Asian or Asian British									
Bangladeshi	10.2	9.1	19.3	0.8	10.4	9.1	19.5	0.9	1.0
Indian	32.9	22	54.9	2.4	31.5	21.0	52.5	2.3	-4.4
Pakistani	32.2	22.2	54.4	2.4	30.8	22.1	52.8	2.3	−2.9
Any other Asian background	14.3	13.7	27.9	1.2	14.8	12.9	27.8	1.2	−0.4
Black or black British									
African	35.6	25.5	61.1	2.7	39.6	27.0	66.6	2.9	9.0
Caribbean	27.3	16.7	43.9	1.9	27.6	17.4	44.9	2.0	2.3
Any other black background	7.6	5.3	12.9	0.6	8.0	5.5	13.5	0.6	4.7
Chinese	9	4.7	13.7	0.6	9.0	4.6	13.6	0.6	−0.7
Mixed									
White and Asian	3.7	3.2	6.9	0.3	4.1	3.5	7.5	0.3	8.7
White and black African	3.9	2.9	6.8	0.3	4.3	3.1	7.4	0.3	8.8
White and black Caribbean	7.4	4.9	12.3	0.5	8.4	5.6	13.9	0.6	13.0
Any other mixed background	5.6	3.4	9.0	0.4	6.4	4.0	10.4	0.5	15.6
White									
British	1,068.2	654.9	1,723.1	75.2	1,037.4	638.5	1,675.9	74.2	−2.7
Irish	9.4	6	15.4	0.7	9.1	5.7	14.8	0.7	−3.9
Any other white background	46.1	24.9	71.0	3.1	57.3	29.7	87.0	3.9	22.5
Any other	27.7	21.5	49.2	2.1	29.1	21.2	50.3	2.2	2.2
Not known/not provided	63.1	46	109.1	4.8	59.7	40.0	99.7	4.4	−8.6
Total	1,404.3	886.6	2,290.9	100.0	1,387.5	870.7	2,258.2	100.0	−1.4

Source: LSC, 2005b

Areas of study, 2003–04

The most popular areas of learning followed by
learners in further education in England in October
2004 were information & communication
technology, health, social care & public services and
foundation programmes (Figure 48).

Sex differences in subject choice

Different subjects attract different proportions of
male and female student. The most sex-segregated
subjects are construction & engineering and
technology & manufacturing, which attract over 90
per cent of male students, and hairdressing &
beauty therapy, which attracts over 90 per cent of
female students.

Figure 48: **Areas of study in FE by sex, England, 2004**

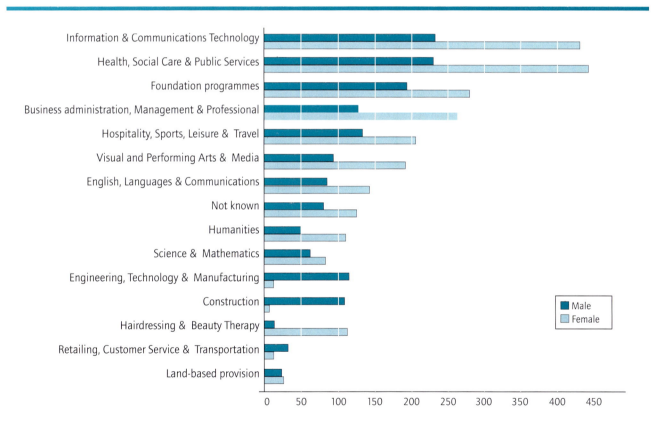

Source: LSC, 2004d

Adult and Community Learning

On 1 October 2003 (figures for 2004 not available at time of writing) in England:

- total of 444,000 learners were enrolled on LSC-funded adult and community learning (ACL) programmes.
- 77 per cent of learners were female, and 23 per cent male.
- 33 per cent of learners were aged 60 and over.
- 85 per cent of learners in adult and community learning were recorded as being of white ethnicity and 7 per cent from ethnic minorities. (Information on ethnicity was not available for the remaining 8 per cent of learners.) (Tables 72 and 73).

The most popular areas of learning for LSC-funded ACL in 2004 were visual and performing arts & media (35 per cent) and hospitality, sports, leisure & travel (31 per cent).

Success rates in further education

In further education in England, 'success rates' reflect both improvements in pass rates and the success of providers in ensuring that learners complete their programmes. Success rates are expressed as retention rate multiplied by achievement (of qualification) rate.

Retention rates

Retention rates increased by 1 percentage point between 2002–03 and 2003–04.

Overall retention rates between 2002–03 and 2003–04 were higher for younger adults on long courses and higher for those aged 19+ on long and short courses in external institutions (Tables 74 and 75).

Table 72: **Learners on LSC-funded ACL provision, by age and sex, England, 2003**

Age	Female	Male	All	% of total
	(Thousands)			
Under 19	5.9	3.0	8.9	2.0
19–24	12.3	3.6	15.9	3.6
25–29	18.9	5.0	23.9	5.4
30–34	26.3	7.1	33.3	7.5
35.39	29.9	8.3	38.2	8.6
40–44	29.4	8.6	38.0	8.6
45–49	27.9	8.2	36.2	8.2
50–54	31.4	8.6	40.0	9.0
55–59	36.6	10.5	47.0	10.6
60+	109.5	36.3	145.9	32.9
Unknown	12.4	3.9	16.3	3.7
Total	340.50	103.10	443.60	100.0

Source: LSC, 2005b

Table 73: **Learners on LSC-funded ACL, by ethnicity and sex, England, 2003**

Ethnicity	Female	Male	All	% of total
	(Thousands)			
Asian or Asian British				
Bangladeshi	1.1	0.3	1.4	0.3
Indian	4.5	1.1	5.7	1.3
Pakistani	2.9	0.5	3.4	0.8
Any other Asian background	1.8	0.5	2.4	0.5
Black or black British				
African	2.2	0.8	3.0	0.7
Caribbean	3.4	0.9	4.3	1.0
Any other black background	0.9	0.3	1.2	0.3
Chinese	1.2	0.4	1.6	0.4
Mixed				
White and Asian	0.4	0.1	0.6	0.1
White and black African	0.3	0.1	0.4	0.1
White and black Caribbean	0.5	0.1	0.6	0.1
Any other mixed background	0.8	0.2	1.0	0.2
White				
British	277.3	84.1	361.4	81.5
Irish	2.8	0.8	3.6	0.8
Any other white background	9.8	2.5	12.3	2.8
Any other	3.5	1.1	4.6	1.0
Not known/not provided	27.2	9.1	36.3	8.2
Total	340.5	103.1	443.6	100.0

Source: LSC, 2005d

Table 74: **Retention rates, by age group and length of qualification, England, 2003–04**

Age	Total FE		External Institutions		Difference from FE benchmark	
	(%)					
	Long	Short	Long	Short	Long	Short
16–18	81	93	71	86	−10	−7
19+	72	93	76	89	+4	−4

Source: LSC, 2005c

Table 75: **Retention rates, by institution type, age group, qualification length, England 2002–04**

Institution type		2002–03						2003–04					
		Long		Short		All		Long		Short		All	
	Age[a]	%	Starts	%	Starts	%	Starts	%	Starts	%	Starts	%	Starts
			(Thousands)		(Thousands)		(Thousands)		(Thousands)		(Thousands)		(Thousands)
General FE and Tertiary Colleges excluding high WP (206 Colleges)	16–18	75	698	91	181	79	879	77	675	93	194	81	869
	19+	70	1,074	93	1,550	83	2,624	72	1,014	94	1,617	85	2,630
	All	72	1,772	93	1,731	82	3,504	74	1,689	94	1,811	84	3,500
General FE and Tertiary Colleges high WP (55 Colleges)	16–18	74	186	89	64	78	250	76	184	92	70	80	255
	19+	71	354	91	550	83	904	73	313	92	547	85	860
	All	72	540	90	614	82	1,153	74	497	92	617	84	1,114
General FE and Tertiary Colleges All (261 Colleges)	16–18	75	884	91	245	79	1,129	77	860	93	264	81	1,124
	19+	70	1,427	92	2,100	83	3,528	72	1,327	93	2,163	85	3,490
	All	72	2,312	92	2,345	82	4,657	74	2,187	93	2,428	84	4,614
Sixth Form Colleges (103 Colleges)	16–18	89	482	94	18	89	501	89	502	94	23	90	525
	19+	72	46	91	75	84	122	73	45	91	85	85	131
	All	87	529	92	94	88	622	88	547	92	108	89	655
Specialist Colleges (24 Colleges)	16–18	79	19	97	7	84	26	79	19	96	8	84	27
	19+	67	22	97	45	87	68	66	29	96	45	85	74
	All	73	41	97	53	86	94	72	48	96	53	85	101
All Further Education Colleges (388 Colleges)	16–18	80	1,386	91	270	82	1,656	81	1,380	93	296	83	1,676
	19+	70	1,496	92	2,221	83	3,717	72	1,401	93	2,293	85	3,694
	All	75	2,882	92	2,491	83	5,373	77	2,781	93	2,589	85	5,370
External institutions (161 Institutions)	16–18	68	10	82	12	75	21	71	10	86	11	79	21
	19+	75	222	86	316	82	538	76	214	89	301	84	514
	All	75	231	86	328	82	559	76	224	89	311	84	535
Total All (549 Institutions)	16–18	80	1,395	91	282	82	1,677	81	1,390	93	307	83	1,696
	19+	71	1,718	92	2,537	83	4,255	72	1,615	93	2,594	85	4,209
	All	75	3,113	92	2,819	83	5,932	77	3,005	93	2,900	84	5,905

Data within the table covers 97% of FE learning aims. The number of starts is shown to give an indication of the relative weightings between cohorts it does not show the complete number of FE starts for that year. Totals may not equal the sum of columns due to rounding.

a   A learner's age is calculated from their age as at 31 August in the academic year they started their qualification.

Source: LSC, 2005c

Overall success rates

FE college success rates have risen considerably in England since 1997–98 (Figure 49).

- Between 2002–03 and 2003–04 overall success rates in further education increased by 3.7 percentage points to over 71 per cent – an increase for the sixth successive year.
- The improvement in overall success rates from 2002–03 to 2003–04 by type of institution was: 3.9 percentage points for general FE colleges, 1.7 percentage points for sixth form colleges and 3.7 percentage points for external institutions. Success rates in specialist colleges remained unchanged (LSC, 2005c).
- Success rates for long and short qualifications increased by 3.3 and 3.4 percentage points to 61.5 per cent and 81.2 per cent respectively.
- In 2003–04, success rates for long qualifications at Levels 1 and 2 increased by 3 or 4 percentage points across all qualification types. For Level 3 qualification, the increase in success rates was 2 percentage points.
- There was a significant increase in the success rate of full Level 2 long qualifications between 2001–02 and 2003–04 and a 5 percentage point increase in full Level 2 success rates for all age groups from 52 per cent in 2002–03 to 57 per cent in 2003–04 (Table 76).

Figure 49: **FE college success rates, England, 1997–2003**

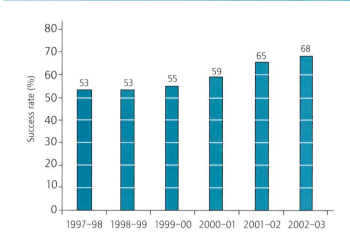

Source: LSC, 2005d

Table 76: **Success rate of full Level 2 qualifications, England, 2001–04**

| Age | 2001–02 | | | | 2002–03 | | | | 2003–04 | | | |
| | Level 2 (long) | | Of which full Level 2 | | Level 2 (long) | | Of which full Level 2 | | Level 2 (long) | | Of which full Level 2 | |
	(%)	No. of starts (Thousands)	(%)	No. of starts (Thousands)	(%)	No. of starts (Thousands)	(%)	No. of starts (Thousands)	(%)	No. of starts (Thousands)	(%)	No. of starts (Thousands)
16–18	53	344	50	100	55	330	52	113	60	322	58	112
19+	49	526	47	118	50	494	51	125	53	483	56	135
All ages	51	870	48	227	52	825	52	238	56	805	57	247

Source: LSC, 2005c

Variations between student groups and course types
Variations in success rates are found among different student cohorts and on different types of course:

- Younger learners on long courses have a higher success rate (81 per cent in 2002–03) than adults on long courses (75 per cent in 2002–03).
- The GCE A/AS-level success rate is 75 per cent for 16–18 year olds but only 54 per cent for adults (LSC Benchmarking Data 2000–01 to 2002–03: http://benchmarkingdata.lsc. gov.uk /year7/index.cfm).
- In 2003–04, achievement rates for short qualifications in external institutions increased by 5 per cent for 16–18 year olds but only 2 per cent for 19+ learners.
- Success rates for adult learners studying for an NVQ Level 2 increased by 4 percentage points to 53 per cent from 2002–03 to 2003–04
- For all ages, females achieve higher success rates in most areas of learning, the exceptions being: 'Land based provision', 'Retailing, Customer Service and Transportation' and 'Health, Social Care and Public Service'.
- The gap in success rates between white and non-white learners has narrowed by nearly 2 percentage points to 4 per cent. Ethnic minorities typically showed an increase of 4 or 5 percentage points whereas the majority 'White' group achieved an increase in success rates of 3 percentage points.
- There have been improvements in success rates of around 3 or 4 percentage points in most areas of learning except construction, where they fell by two percentage points. This has been partly attributed to an increase in the proportion of long programmes being delivered.

Tables 77–81 give breakdowns of success rates according to institution, student characteristics and qualification length.

Table 77: **Success rates in LSC-funded FE provision, by institution type, age group, qualification length and expected end year, England 2002–04**

		Long		Short		All		Long		Short		All	
		%	Starts	%	Starts	%	Starts	%	Starts	%	Starts	%	Starts
			(Thousands)		(Thousands)		(Thousands)		(Thousands)		(Thousands)		(Thousands)
General FE and	16–18	58	698	74	181	61	879	62	675	76	194	65	869
Tertiary Colleges	19+	53	1,074	82	1,550	70	2,624	57	1,014	85	1,617	74	2,630
excluding high WP	All	55	1,772	81	1,731	68	3,504	59	1,689	84	1,811	72	3,500
(206 Colleges)													
General FE and	16–18	55	186	66	64	58	250	58	184	73	70	62	255
Tertiary Colleges	19+	52	354	75	550	66	904	55	313	79	547	70	860
high WP	All	53	540	74	614	64	1,153	56	497	78	617	68	1,114
(55 Colleges)													
General FE and	16–18	58	884	72	245	61	1,129	61	860	76	264	64	1,124
Tertiary Colleges,	19+	53	1,427	80	2,100	69	3,528	56	1,327	83	2,163	73	3,490
All (261 Colleges)	All	55	2,312	79	2,345	67	4,657	58	2,187	82	2,428	71	4,614
Sixth Form	16–18	78	482	73	18	78	501	79	502	76	23	79	525
Colleges	19+	55	46	80	75	70	122	56	45	81	85	73	131
(103 Colleges)	All	76	529	79	94	76	622	77	547	80	108	78	655
All Further	16–18	63	19	80	7	68	26	63	19	85	8	70	27
Education Colleges	19+	51	22	85	45	74	68	51	29	88	45	73	74
(24 Colleges)	All	57	41	84	53	72	94	55	48	88	53	72	101
Specialist	16–18	65	1,386	72	270	66	1,656	68	1,380	76	296	69	1,676
Colleges	19+	53	1,496	80	2,221	69	3,717	56	1,401	83	2,293	73	3,694
(388 Colleges)	All	58	2,882	79	2,491	68	5,373	62	2,781	82	2,589	72	5,370
External	16–18	49	10	62	12	56	21	52	10	70	11	62	21
Insitutions	19+	55	222	67	316	62	538	58	214	71	301	65	514
(161 Institutions)	All	55	231	67	328	62	559	58	224	71	311	65	535
Total All	16–18	65	1,395	72	282	66	1,677	67	1,390	76	307	69	1,696
	19+	53	1,718	78	2,537	68	4,255	56	1,615	82	2,594	72	4,209
(549 Institutions)	All	58	3,113	78	2,819	67	5,932	61	3,005	81	2,900	71	5,905

Data within the table cover 97% of FE learning aims. The number of starts is shown to give an indication of the relative weightings between cohorts; it does not show the complete number of FE starts for that year. Totals may not equal the sum of columns due to rounding.

a   A learner's age is calculated from their age as at 31 August in the academic year they started their qualification.

Source: LSC, 2005c

Table 78: **Success rates in LSC-funded FE provision, by area of learning, qualification length and expected end year, England 2002–2004**

	2002–2003						2003–2004					
	Long		Short		All		Long		Short		All	
	%	Starts	%	Starts	%	Starts	%	Starts	%	Starts	%	Starts
		(Thousands)		(Thousands)		(Thousands)		(Thousands)		(Thousands)		(Thousands)
Business Administration, Management and Professional	54	358	69	221	60	579	57	316	72	197	63	514
Construction	43	85	87	72	63	157	47	91	87	51	61	142
Engineering, Technology and Manufacturing	51	117	75	62	59	179	53	105	78	60	62	165
English, Languages and Communications	64	281	64	93	64	374	67	275	72	96	68	371
Foundation Programmes	63	307	72	466	68	773	65	340	75	548	71	888
Hairdressing and Beauty Therapy	59	110	69	81	63	191	61	98	75	63	67	161
Health, Social Care and Public Services	55	206	89	555	79	762	56	212	91	586	82	798
Hospitality, Sports Leisure and Travel	59	163	84	304	75	467	62	169	86	341	78	510
Humanities	68	343	71	57	68	400	71	336	77	46	72	382
Information and Communication Technology	46	449	70	435	58	884	48	391	74	421	62	812
Land-based provision	54	41	81	44	68	85	57	43	84	41	70	84
Retailing, Customer Service and Transportation	57	40	82	54	71	94	59	35	83	44	72	79
Science and Mathematics	64	251	73	62	66	313	67	240	76	42	68	281
Visual & Performing Arts and Media	65	311	77	145	69	455	69	309	82	170	74	479
Unspecified area of learning	57	51	91	170	83	220	73	43	93	196	89	239
Total	58	3,113	78	2,819	67	5,932	61	3,005	81	2,900	71	5,905

Data within the table cover 97% of FE learning aims. The number of starts is shown to give an indication of the relative weightings between cohorts it does not show the complete number of FE starts for that year. Totals may not equal the sum of columns due to rounding.

Source: LSC, 2005c

Table 79: **Success rates in LSC-funded FE provision, by sex and expected end year, England 2002–04**

Area of learning	2002–03						2003–04					
	Male		Female		All		Male		Female		All	
	%	Starts	%	Starts	%	Starts	%	Starts	%	Starts	%	Starts
		(Thousands)		(Thousands)		(Thousands)		(Thousands)		(Thousands)		(Thousands)
Business Administration, Management and Professional	61	397	58	182	60	579	63	349	62	165	63	514
Construction	60	9	63	148	63	157	61	8	61	134	61	142
Engineering, Technology and Manufacturing	67	23	58	156	59	179	68	19	62	146	62	165
English, Languages and Communications	65	236	61	138	64	374	70	235	66	136	68	371
Foundation Programmes	69	449	66	324	68	773	72	524	70	364	71	888
Hairdressing and Beauty Therapy	64	164	57	27	63	191	67	147	60	15	67	161
Health, Social Care and Public Services	76	498	86	263	79	762	79	516	87	282	82	798
Hospitality, Sports Leisure and Travel	78	283	72	184	75	467	80	307	74	203	78	510
Humanities	69	254	67	146	68	400	73	242	70	140	72	382
Information and Communication Technology	59	521	56	363	58	884	63	480	61	332	62	812
Land-based provision	66	44	70	41	68	85	68	45	72	39	70	84
Retailing, Customer Service and Transportation	70	55	74	39	71	94	71	45	75	34	72	79
Science and Mathematics	67	170	64	143	66	313	69	156	68	126	68	281
Visual & Performing Arts and Media	70	300	66	156	69	455	75	316	70	163	74	479
Unspecified area of learning	84	133	82	87	83	220	89	143	88	95	89	239
Total	68	3,534	66	2,398	67	5,932	72	3,530	70	2,375	71	5,905

Data within the table cover 97% of FE learning aims. The number of starts is shown to give an indication of the relative weightings between cohorts; it does not show the complete number of FE starts for that year. Totals may not equal the sum of columns due to rounding.

Source: LSC, 2005c

Table 80: **Success rates in LSC-funded FE provision, by ethnicity, sex and expected end year, England 2002–04**

Ethnicity	2002–03						2003–04					
	Female		Male		All		Female		Male		All	
	%	Starts	%	Starts	%	Starts	%	Starts	%	Starts	%	Starts
		(Thousands)		(Thousands)		(Thousands)		(Thousands)		(Thousands)		(Thousands)
Bangladeshi	69	28	61	25	65	53	72	31	67	28	70	59
Indian	69	85	65	56	67	141	72	90	68	60	71	150
Pakistani	66	86	59	58	63	143	70	89	64	59	67	148
Other – Asian	67	42	62	43	64	85	71	44	67	42	69	86
Black African	64	89	59	69	62	158	68	109	64	77	66	186
Black Caribbean	60	62	54	38	58	100	63	64	59	40	62	104
Black other	59	20	55	14	58	34	63	19	62	14	63	33
Chinese	67	31	62	19	65	50	71	31	69	19	70	51
White	69	2,717	68	1,781	69	4,498	73	2,761	71	1,809	72	4,570
Other	64	121	60	98	62	219	68	134	65	102	67	236
Not known/not provided	65	254	64	196	64	450	70	158	70	125	70	283
Total	68	3,534	66	2,398	67	5,932	72	3,530	70	2,375	71	5,905

Data within the table cover 97% of FE learning aims. The number of starts is shown to give an indication of the relative weightings between cohorts it does not show the complete number of FE starts for that year. Totals may not equal the sum of columns due to rounding.

Source: LSC, 2005c

Table 81: **Success rates in LSC-funded FE provision, by disability, sex and expected end year, England 2002–04**

Disability	Age[a]	2002–03						2003–04					
		Female		Male		All		Female		Male		All	
		%	Starts	%	Starts	%	Starts	%	Starts	%	Starts	%	Starts
			(Thousands)		(Thousands)		(Thousands)		(Thousands)		(Thousands)		(Thousands)
Has disability	16–18	67	82	63	93	65	175	70	94	67	107	68	201
	19+	69	210	68	173	68	383	72	237	72	194	72	431
	All	68	292	66	266	67	558	72	331	70	301	71	631
No disability	16–18	69	665	63	570	66	1,235	71	696	66	601	69	1,296
	19+	69	1,914	68	1,096	68	3,010	73	1,996	72	1,134	72	3,130
	All	69	2,579	66	1,666	68	4,245	72	2,692	70	1,735	71	4,427
No information	16–18	67	140	61	127	64	268	71	105	66	95	68	200
	19+	68	523	68	339	68	862	70	403	70	245	70	648
	All	68	663	66	466	67	1,129	70	508	69	340	70	848
Total	16–18	68	887	63	790	66	1,677	71	895	66	802	69	1,696
	19+	68	2,647	68	1,608	68	4,255	72	2,636	72	1,573	72	4,209
	All	68	3,534	66	2,398	67	5,932	72	3,530	70	2,375	71	5,905

Data within the table cover 97% of FE learning aims. The number of starts is shown to give an indication of the relative weightings between cohorts; it does not show the complete number of FE starts for that year. Totals may not equal the sum of columns due to rounding.

a A learner's age is calculated from their age as at 31 August in the academic year they started their qualification.

Source: LSC, 2005c

Students involved in open and distance learning[10] (ODL) consistently have lower retention and success rates than those engaged in conventional education. The difference increases for older learners, suggesting that older learners experience more difficulty with ODL than younger ones

Skills for Life (SfL)

Skills for Life, launched in 2001, is the government's strategy for improving the English adult population's skills in literacy, numeracy and English for speakers of other languages (ESOL). SfL targets are that 1.5 million adults will achieve the national certificates in literacy and numeracy by 2007 and 2.25 million by 2010.

Progress towards the targets

- The number of adult learners contributing to *Skills for Life* targets increased by 27 per cent in 2003–04, with an estimated 2.1 million people having taken part in literacy and numeracy learning. More than half of these were 16–18 year olds (DfES, 2004c).
- A National Audit Office study indicates that the 2004 target of increasing the skills of 750,000 people has been achieved (NAO, 2004). However:
- A joint survey by Ofsted and the ALI found that ESOL was one of the weakest areas, and that basic skills teaching was also weak in the criminal justice system and on vocational programmes (ALI, 2003).

5.3 Local Education Authority provision

Local Education Authorities have traditionally had an important role in providing education opportunities for adults.

Participation

In November 2003, there were over 1 million enrolments in adult and community education courses provided by Local Education Authorities (LEAs) in England, nearly three-quarters of which were by women.

Enrolments on daytime classes increased from 504,000 in November 1992 to 580,000 in November 2002. Over the same period, evening and open distance-learning course enrolments fell from 775,000 to 461,000.

Since 2000, enrolments on daytime courses have outnumbered those for evening and open distance-learning courses. In November 2002 the majority of enrolments (660,000) were for courses that did not lead to any formal qualification.

Funding

The key policy drivers affecting LEA provision for adults funded by the LSC remain the priorities outlined in the Skills Strategy especially Skills for Life and the Level 2 entitlement although there is also a funding safeguard for personal and community development.

LEAs are also expected to respond to LSC priorities regarding widening Adult Participation, equality and Diversity, e-learning and -the LSC's strategy for working with the voluntary and community sector.

In the annual fee survey conducted by NIACE in 2004, nearly a half of responding LEAs secure the provision of adult learning primarily through direct delivery, 19 per cent primarily through contracts and service level agreements and 32 per cent through a combination of these (NIACE, 2005).

The mean average fees charged during 2003–04 were:

- £1.38/hour for accredited and qualification bearing provision in LEAs.
- £1.87/hour for non-accredited and internally accredited provision in LEAs.

The most generous concessions tend to be given to those on unemployment and means-tested benefits.

Curriculum

Many local authorities offer a range of traditional general education provision, including arts, crafts, modern languages, Keep Fit and self-development programmes. Foreign languages and the creative arts are a strong element in many LEA adult-learning services.

A survey of language provision by LEAs carried out by CILT, the National Centre for Languages, in 2004–05 found that there were 36 different languages on offer to adult learners in 69 responding LEAs. A third of all language learners were studying Spanish and over a quarter French and about a tenth Italian.

Three-quarters (74 per cent) of all language learners were studying at Entry Level and Level 1. Very few learners (1 per cent) were reported at Level 4 and above.

Inspectorate views of LEA provision are to be found in Section 6 'Quality issues'.

5.4 Learndirect[11]

Over 1.2 million people enrolled on 2.5 million learndirect courses between 2000 and 2004. About 15 per cent of these were either unemployed or returning to work after time out of the workplace

During Adult Learners' Week 2005, the learndirect website received 239,000 hits, an increase of 70 per cent.

- 27 per cent of calls to the advice line during the week specifically mentioned the ALW campaign.
- 45 per cent of callers had a highest-level qualification of Level 2 or below.
- 59 per cent of callers were aged 25–49.
- 38 per cent of callers were not in employment or unemployed.
- Nearly 77 per cent of callers were currently not in learning.
- 2,203 callers had agreed to be contacted again for post-helpline research.
  (NIACE, Adult Learners' Week 2005: Review of Activity

5.5 Programmes funded by the European Social Fund (ESF)

A government researcher has supplied an estimate of minimum numbers of learners on ESF programmes. He estimates that there were around 158,000 adult learners in 2003, and, around 284,000 in 2004, with the following proviso:

> These figures are assumed to be underestimates as they relate only to the number of learners in completed ESF projects during the years in question. They do not include adult learners who were on ESF projects that were ongoing during those years but had not completed by the end of the year. The figures also relate only to those projects under the ESF Lifelong Learning priority. There are five priorities under ESF and the other priorities will embrace beneficiaries who will have undertaken one or more formal learning episodes during their time on projects.

Section 6
Work-related education and training

6.1 Work-based learning (WBL)

Work-based learning options are available to young people in England and Wales who decide not to continue in full-time education. WBL includes apprenticeships providing structured learning programmes for young people aged 16 to 24, combining work-based training with off-the-job learning.

According to the LSC (LSC, 2005b), a total of 320,000 people were participating in WBL in England in October 2004 – an increase of 1 per cent over 2003.

Table 82 shows trends in participation in work-based learning between summer 2000 and summer 2004. The table shows a steady increase in take-up of lower-level apprenticeships and Entry to

Table 82: **Starts in LSC-funded work-based learning provision, by age group and programme type, England, 2003–04**

Year		Advanced Apprenticeship	Apprenticeship	NVQ Learning	E2E[a]	WBL for young people
				(Thousands)		
2000–2001	30 Jul 2000–29 Oct 2000	28.2	33.6	18.5	6.9	87.2
	30 Oct 2000–28 Jan 2001	16.1	20.2	9.6	6.0	51.9
	29 Jan 2001–28 Apr 2001	14.2	23.9	10.4	6.4	54.9
	29 Apr 2001–28 July 2001	13.8	26.5	11.7	7.1	59.0
	Total	72.4	104.1	50.1	26.3	252.9
2001–2002	30 Jul 2001–28 Oct 2001	23.7	38.3	14.5	9.0	85.5
	29 Oct 2001–27 Jan 2002	11.2	21.6	10.2	6.7	49.7
	28 Jan 2002–28 Apr 2002	9.8	22.8	13.1	7.2	52.8
	29 Apr 2002–28 July 2002	9.4	25.6	16.3	8.3	59.6
	Total	54.0	108.3	54.1	31.1	247.6
2002–2003	28 Jul 2002–27 Oct 2002	21.7	41.0	12.9	9.2	84.8
	28 Oct 2002–26 Jan 2003	9.8	23.5	8.7	7.4	49.3
	27 Jan 2003–27 Apr 2003	8.2	24.6	9.1	8.3	50.1
	28 Apr 2003–27 July 2003	7.6	26.7	10.0	–	–
	Total	47.3	115.7	40.6	35.7	239.3
2003–2004	1 Aug 2003–31 Oct 2003	25.8	54.4	9.7	22.3	112.2
	1 Nov 2003–31 Jan 2004	10.8	26.6	5.9	12.5	55.8
	1 Feb 2004–30 Apr 2004	9.9	27.8	6.0	12.4	56.2
	1 May 2004–31 July 2004	9.3	27.6	5.0	13.9	55.8
	Total	55.9	136.5	26.6	61.1	280.0
2004–2005	1 Aug 2004–31 Oct 2004	23.5	54.9	5.4	15.4	99.3

a Entry to Employment (E2E) was previously referred to as Life Skills and includes Work Based Learning Below Level 2.

Source: LSC, 2005b

Employment programmes but a marked reduction in the numbers engaging in learning for NVQs.

The number learning on apprenticeships in 2004 was 270,000, an increase of 5 per cent over 2003.

The shift towards apprenticeships and away from NVQ learning has continued, with a sharp decrease in the numbers involved in learning for NVQs since 2003. However, there has been a 9 per cent decrease in the numbers entering Entry to Employment (E2E) programmes since October 2003.[12]

The most popular area of learning in WBL was engineering, yechnology & manufacturing (23 per cent).

6.2 Characteristics of WBL learners

In October 2004:
- About 64 per cent of WBL learners were aged under 19, an increase of 2 per cent on 2003.
- 59 per cent of WBL learners were male and 41 per cent female.
- 93 per cent of WBL learners were recorded as being of white ethnicity and 6 per cent from ethnic minorities (information was not available for the remaining 1 per cent).

6.3 Modern Apprenticeships

At the end of 2004, there were 255,500 trainees (compared with 75,800 in 1997):
- 4 per cent of trainees were from black and ethnic minorities (although they make up 13.5 per cent of all 16–24 year olds).
- Men took 59 per cent of all apprenticeships and women 41%.

6.4 Entry to Employment (E2E)

In 2003–04, 60,000 young adults enrolled in E2E of whom:
- 38 per cent were women
- 33 per cent had a disability
- 17 per cent were from ethnic minorities. (LSC, 2004b)

6.5 Success rates in work-based learning

Between 2002–03 and 2003 –04:
- Overall success rates for learners who left learning with a full framework or an NVQ only, increased from 41 per cent to 46 per cent. The figures cover all ages and NVQs at all levels as well as apprenticeship frameworks and qualifications that count towards the LSC's targets for attainment of young people.
- Within advanced apprenticeships, framework completion rates (the percentage of learners leaving apprenticeships having achieved the full framework) increased by one percentage point.
- Within apprenticeships at Level 2, framework completion rates increased by six percentage points, while completion rates for all apprentice-ships increased by four percentage points.
- Success rates within NVQ training at Level 2 increased by 9 percentage points for 16–18-year-olds and for all age groups by 8 percentage points. (The number of learners leaving NVQ training fell significantly and this can distort comparisons of success rates.)
- Success rates in apprenticeships at Level 2 improved for all areas of learning. Engineering, technology and manufacturing was the only area of learning within Advanced Apprenticeship not to show an increase in success rate.

(NB: 25 per cent of the National Vocational Qualification funding in 2005–06 will only be paid when young people complete their apprenticeship framework (complete their full training programme) – this provides a clear incentive for providers to improve their achievement rates.)

Tables 83–5 show success rates by programme type, area of learning and learner characteristics. They show that success rates tend to be higher for the sexes in the areas in which they predominate (e.g. for women in hairdressing, for men in construction).

They also show some ethnic differences. White apprentices were most likely to complete the advanced apprenticeship framework, followed by Indian and Pakistani trainees. In 2003–04, Chinese and white groups were most successful in completing the framework at Level 2 and gaining NVQs.

Table 83: **Success rates in LSC-funded work-based learning provision, by age group and programme type, England, 2003–04**

Programme type	Age[a]	Framework completion rate	NVQ only[b]	NVQ success rate	Total leavers
			(%)		(Numbers)
Advanced Apprenticeships	16–18	36	13	49	23,800
	19+	29	15	44	27,500
	All	32	14	46	51,400
Apprenticeships (at level 2)	16–18	31	12	43	65,300
	19+	29	14	42	41,500
	All	30	12	43	106,800
All Apprenticeships	16–18	33	12	45	89,100
	19+	29	14	43	69,100
	All	31	13	44	158,200
NVQ Training 1	16–18	–	54	54	100
	19+	–	49	49	400
	All	–	50	50	500
NVQ Training 2	16–18	–	52	52	12,900
	19+	–	63	63	9,800
	All	–	57	57	22,700
NVQ Training 3	16–18	–	51	51	1,500
	19+	–	55	55	3,400
	All	–	54	54	5,000
NVQ Training 4	16–18	–	71	71	100
	19+	–	73	73	1,100
	All	–	73	73	1,200
All frameworks or NVQs	16–18	–	–	46	103,700
	19+	–	–	46	83,800
	All	–	–	46	187,500

a In Work-based Learning, a learner's age is age at the start of learning.
b Early apprenticeship leavers who achieved an NVQ but no framework.

Source: LSC, 2005c

Table 84a: **Success rates in LSC-funded work-based learning provision, by area of learning, sex and programme type, England, 2003–04**

Area of learning	Sex	Advanced Apprenticeships			
		Framework completion rate	NVQ only[a]	NVQ success rate	Total leavers
			(%)		(Numbers)
Business Administration Management & Professional	Female	35	19	53	5,100
	Male	34	13	47	1,800
	All	35	17	52	6,900
Construction	Female	36	21	–	–
	Male	27	32	59	5,200
	All	27	32	59	5,200
Engineering, Technology & Manufacturing	Female	35	5	40	300
	Male	43	7	50	14,300
	All	43	7	50	14,600
English, Languages & Communication	Female	–	–	–	–
	Male	–	–	–	–
	All	–	–	–	–
Foundation Programmes	Female	–	–	–	–
	Male	–	–	–	–
	All	–	–	–	–
Hairdressing & Beauty Therapy	Female	36	11	47	2,300
	Male	28	4	31	100
	All	35	10	46	2,500
Health, Social Care & Public Services	Female	24	23	47	6,200
	Male	21	13	33	500
	All	24	22	46	6,700
Hospitality, Sports Leisure & Travel	Female	28	8	36	3,800
	Male	15	7	22	2,800
	All	22	8	30	6,600
Humanities	Female	–	–	–	–
	Male	–	–	–	–
	All	–	–	–	–
Information & Communication Technology	Female	50	5	56	200
	Male	50	6	56	1,200
	All	50	6	56	1,400
Land-based provision	Female	35	12	46	300
	Male	42	15	58	400
	All	39	14	53	700
Retailing, Customer Service and Transportation	Female	26	15	40	4,100
	Male	21	11	32	2,400
	All	24	13	37	6,500
Science & Maths	Female	–	–	–	–
	Male	–	–	–	–
	All	49	9	58	100
Visual & Performing Arts & Media	Female	46	19	–	–
	Male	34	24	58	300
	All	35	23	59	300
Unspecified AOL	Female	–	–	–	–
	Male	–	–	–	–
	All	–	–	–	–
Total	Female	29	16	45	22,300
	Male	35	13	47	29,100
	All	32	14	46	51,400

a Early apprenticeship leavers who achieved an NVQ but no framework

Source: LSC, 2005c

Table 84b: **Success rates in LSC-funded work-based learning provision by area of learning, sex and programme type, England, 2003–04**

Area of learning	Sex	Apprenticeships (at Level 2)			
		Framework completion rate	NVQ only[a]	NVQ success rate	Total leavers
			(%)		(Numbers)
Business Administration Management & Professional	Female	41	11	52	11,900
	Male	36	9	45	3,900
	All	40	11	51	15,800
Construction	Female	20	9	29	100
	Male	25	13	38	10,800
	All	25	13	38	10,900
Engineering, Technology & Manufacturing	Female	32	15	47	400
	Male	30	12	42	9,000
	All	30	12	42	9,400
English, Languages & Communication	Female	–	–	–	–
	Male	–	–	–	–
	All	–	–	–	–
Foundation Programmes	Female	–	–	–	–
	Male	–	–	–	–
	All	–	–	–	–
Hairdressing & Beauty Therapy	Female	38	6	44	9,100
	Male	20	6	26	800
	All	36	6	43	9,900
Health, Social Care & Public Services	Female	16	22	38	10,500
	Male	18	15	33	1,100
	All	17	21	38	11,600
Hospitality, Sports Leisure & Travel	Female	30	13	42	9,300
	Male	23	14	37	9,000
	All	26	13	40	18,300
Humanities	Female	–	–	–	–
	Male	–	–	–	–
	All	–	–	–	–
Information & Communication Technology	Female	56	7	64	600
	Male	51	14	65	2,900
	All	52	13	65	3,500
Land-based provision	Female	38	12	50	1,200
	Male	34	16	50	1,500
	All	36	14	50	2,700
Retailing, Customer Service & Transportation	Female	31	11	42	15,100
	Male	27	11	38	9,400
	All	30	11	40	24,500
Science & Maths	Female	–	–	–	–
	Male	–	–	–	–
	All	–	–	–	–
Visual & Performing Arts & Media	Female	–	–	–	–
	Male	24	30	53	100
	All	28	23	50	200
Unspecified AOL	Female	–	–	–	–
	Male	–	–	–	–
	All	29	24	53	100
Total	Female	32	12	44	58,300
	Male	28	12	41	48,500
	All	30	12	43	106,800

b Early apprenticeship leavers who achieved an NVQ but no framework

Source: LSC, 2005c

Table 84c: **Success rates in LSC-funded work-based learning provision, by area of learning, sex and programme type, England, 2003–04**

Area of learning	Sex	NVQ Training		All frameworks of NVQs	
		NVQ success rate	Total leavers rate	NVQ success rate	Total leavers
		(%)	(Numbers)	(%)	(Numbers)
Business Administration Management & Professional	Female	57	3,200	53	20,200
	Male	51	1,600	47	7,300
	All	55	4,800	52	27,500
Construction	Female	–	–	34	200
	Male	46	1,400	45	17,300
	All	45	1,400	45	17,500
Engineering, Technology & Manufacturing	Female	73	300	53	900
	Male	62	4,500	49	27,800
	All	62	4,800	49	28,700
English, Languages & Communication	Female	–	–	–	–
	Male	–	–	–	–
	All	–	–	–	–
Foundation Programmes	Female	–	–	–	–
	Male	–	–	–	–
	All	–	–	–	–
Hairdressing & Beauty Therapy	Female	50	1,000	45	12,500
	Male	39	100	27	1,000
	All	49	1,100	44	13,400
Health, Social Care & Public Services	Female	51	6,100	44	22,800
	Male	73	3,100	60	4,700
	All	58	9,200	47	27,500
Hospitality, Sports Leisure & Travel	Female	49	600	41	13,600
	Male	47	1,000	34	12,800
	All	48	1,600	38	26,500
Humanities	Female	–	–	–	–
	Male	–	–	–	–
	All	–	–	–	–
Information & Communication Technology	Female	68	200	63	1,000
	Male	56	500	62	4,600
	All	59	700	62	5,700
Land-based provision	Female	73	700	57	2,200
	Male	49	400	51	2,300
	All	64	1,100	54	4,600
Retailing, Customer Service & Transportation	Female	56	2,200	43	21,300
	Male	53	2,200	39	14,000
	All	54	4,400	41	35,400
Science & Maths	Female	–	–	57	100
	Male	–	–	57	100
	All	68	100	59	100
Visual & Performing Arts & Media	Female	53	100	52	100
	Male	53	100	56	400
	All	54	100	55	600
Unspecified AOL	Female	–	–	61	100
	Male	–	–	–	–
	All	–	–	56	100
Total	Female	55	14,500	46	95,100
	Male	59	14,800	46	92,500
	All	57	29,300	46	187,500

a Including early apprenticeship leavers who achieved an NVQ but no framework

Source: LSC, 2005c

Table 85: **Success rates in LSC-funded work-based learning provision, by ethnicity and programme type, England, 2003–04**

Ethnicity	Advanced Apprenticeships				Apprenticeships (at Level 2)				NVQ training		All frameworks or NVQ	
	Framework completion rate	NVQ Only[a] (%)	NVQ Success rate (%)	Total Leavers (Number)	Framework completion rate	NVQ Only[a] (%)	NVQ Success rate (%)	Total Leavers (Number)	NVQ Only[a] (%)	Total Leavers (Number)	NVQ Success rate (%)	Total Leavers (Number)
Bangladeshi	23	12	35	100	19	11	30	500	46	400	37	1,000
Indian	27	14	41	300	27	12	39	700	50	300	42	1,400
Pakistani	26	20	46	300	23	11	34	900	49	700	41	2,000
Other – Asian	26	12	38	100	22	15	37	200	47	100	40	400
Black African	17	17	34	100	11	15	26	400	55	200	36	800
Black Caribbean	16	18	35	300	19	13	32	800	56	500	39	1,600
Black other	25	13	38	200	23	17	40	400	52	200	43	700
Chinese	–	–	–	–	33	9	42	100	–	–	53	100
White	32	14	46	48,400	31	12	43	99,900	57	26,000	46	174,300
Other	21	12	33	500	22	10	32	1,600	53	600	37	2,600
Not known/not provided	45	15	60	1,100	32	19	51	1,200	59	300	56	2,700
Total	32	14	46	51,400	30	12	43	106,800	57	29,300	46	187,500

a Early apprenticeship leavers who achieved an NVQ but no framework

Source: LSC 2005c

6.6 Government plans and priorities for work-based learning

WBL-related measures announced by the LSC in 2005 include:

- Funding rates for young people in the 16–18 age group to be increased by 2.5 per cent.
- Increased funding allocations for the continued expansion of the apprenticeships programme and for Entry to Employment (E2E).
- Funding rates for learners aged 19 and over when they start an apprenticeship to be reduced by 6 per cent from 2004–05 levels (providers will be expected to recoup these funds from higher employer contributions).
- The LSC to introduce a 'planned mix of provision' by which local LSCs will be able to increasingly focus local training provision on meeting the skills needs of local employment sectors.

6.7 Job-related training[13]

In the UK, the workplace is one of the most important locations and providers of adult learning. Scottish data from 2003 clearly illustrate this (Table 86).

6.8 Job-related training by country, region and area

In spring 2004:

- 16 per cent of employees of working age (5.1 million people) in the United Kingdom had received some job-related training in the four weeks prior to interview in the Labour Force Survey, about the same proportion as in each of the spring quarters since 1995. In general, greater proportions of women than men received job-related training, and the proportion was lower for older than for younger employees.

Table 86: **Adult participation[a] in education and training, by age, Scotland, 2003**

	16–24	25–34	35–44	45–59	60–64	All
	(%)					
None	46	69	70	78	91	72
On-the-job training	19	19	20	16	3	17
Further education course	10	3	3	2	1	3
A university based course	20	5	2	1	1	4
Distance learning/university	2	3	3	1	1	2
School	4	0	0	0	0	1
Adult education or evening class	2	2	3	2	2	2
Help with reading, writing or use of numbers	0	0	0	0	0	0
Other	1	1	1	1	1	1
Base	1,000	2,057	2,632	3,260	1,089	10,038

Columns add to more than 100% since multiple responses were allowed.

a Adult population aged 16–64 years

Source: Scottish Executive, 2003

- People in Wales were the most likely to have received job-related training followed by England and Scotland. People in Northern Ireland were least likely to have received training (Table 87).
- People in the North East of England were more likely to have received job-related training in the previous four weeks than people in any other region.
- The individual areas with the highest proportions of workers who had received job-related training were Oxford, Wear Valley (North East) and Penwith (South West). The areas with the lowest proportions were all in the East region – Maldon, Suffolk Coastal and St Edmundsbury (Table 88).

In 2004–05, the same pattern is apparent. The North East and Yorkshire and Humber had the highest number of working age people receiving job-related training in the four weeks prior to interview, and the East of England the lowest.

6.9 Employer-provided training in England

The National Employers Skill Survey 2004 (Hogarth *et al*, 2004), found that in England:

- 64 per cent of employers had provided training in the preceding 12 months (about 50 per cent of which was on the job).
- 61 per cent of staff had received some training.
- An average of just under 6 days of training were provided.
- Most training offered was for induction or health and safety.
- In the 2003 NESS survey, just over 50 per cent of employers reported that training led to a formal qualification (LSC, 2005a).

In 2004–05:

- The numbers of adults of working age in England who had received job-related training in the four weeks prior to interview was 16.6 per cent (Table 88).
- The incidence of training was higher for those in professional and associated professional and

Table 87: **Employees and self-employed of working age who received job-related training in the previous four weeks, by region and nation and by highest and lowest unitary authorities/local authority districts, Great Britain, 2003–04**

	(%)	UA/LAD	(%)		(%)
		Highest		Lowest	
England					
North East	16.5	Wear Valley	24.1	Berwick-upon-Tweed	9.8
North West	15.2	South Lakeland	21.5	Warrington	10.3
Yorkshire and the					
Humber	16.5	Hambleton	20.8	Ryedale	9.8
East Midlands	14.7	Bassetlaw	22.6	Corby	7.6
West Midlands	14.9	Shrewsbury	21.8	Redditch	8.9
East	13.2	Cambridge	19.3	Maldon	3.3
London	15.4	Greenwich	22.7	Islington	8.2
South East	15.6	Oxford	24.4	Runnymede	9.7
South West	15.5	Penwith	23.3	East Dorset	8.6
Wales	16.1	Cardiff	19.6	Monmouthshire	12.6
Scotland	16.6	East Dunbarton-		Orkney Islands	8.4
		shire	21.3		

Source: ONS, 2004

Table 88: **Employees receiving job-related training in previous four weeks, England, 2004–05**

	Working age employees	Working age employees receiving job-related training in the last 4 weeks	
	(Thousands)	(Thousands)	(%)
England	19,755	3,281	16.6
North East	970	179	18.4
North West	2,643	429	16.2
Yorkshire & Humberside	2,001	347	17.4
East Midlands	1,707	288	16.8
West Midlands	2,090	332	15.9
East of England	2,256	348	15.4
London 2,774	453	16.3	
South East	3,329	579	17.4
South West	1,983	326	16.4

Source: ONS/English Local Labour Force Survey, 2004–05

technical occupations as well as for those working in personal services occupations.
- Training rates were higher in public services, public administration, education and health occupations than in other sectors (all areas in which women tend to work). Part-time workers tend to receive less training than full-time workers.

6.10 Type and length of training received by group of employees

In spring 2004:
- 7.7 per cent of employees had received only off-the-job training in the last four weeks, 5.3 per cent had received only on-the-job training and 3.2 per cent had received both types of training (Table 91).
- Younger employees tend to have both off-the-job and on-the-job training, while older employees are more likely to participate only in on-the-job training. Over a quarter (27 per cent) of the youngest age group (16–19-year-olds), who recently engaged in training, reported that the training was both on-the-job and off-the-job training, compared to five per cent among 60–64 year olds.

- 38 per cent of trainees between the ages of 60 and 64 years reported that the training was purely on-the-job, compared with 29 per cent of trainees between the ages 16 and 19.

Job-related training by trainee characteristics
Tables 89–91 also show that:
- Employees were more likely to receive job-related training than the self-employed, the unemployed or the economically inactive.
- Overall participation rates were higher amongst women (16 per cent) than men (13 per cent).
- People with high levels of qualifications were much more likely than those with low or no qualifications to have received job-related training.
- 22 per cent of employees of mixed ethnic origin, 19.9 per cent of Black or Black British employees, 16.5 per cent of Chinese employees, and 14.1 per cent of employees of Asian or Asian British origin, had received job-related training compared with 16 per cent of white employees.

Table 89: **Participation in job-related training[a] by employees[b] in the previous four weeks, by type of training and economic characteristics, United Kingdom, 2004**

	Total number of employees	Of which: receiving off-the-job training[c]	receiving on-the-job training	receiving both on- and off-the-job training	receiving any training
	(Thousands)	(%)			
All employees	23,510	7.7	5.3	3.2	16.1
By industry[d]					
Agriculture, forestry & fishing	149	–	–	–	11.7
Energy & water supply	258	8.9	4.8	–	16.5
Manufacturing	3,461	4.2	3.5	1.8	9.5
Construction	1,320	5.9	3.5	3.6	13.0
Distribution, hotels, restaurants	4,769	6.3	3.7	2.0	12.0
Transport	1,619	5.0	5.0	1.5	11.4
Banking, finance & insurance	3.540	7.6	5.3	2.6	15.5
Public administration, education & health	7,169	11.2	7.7	5.2	24.1
Other services	1,212	7.8	5.0	3.4	16.2
By occupation					
Managers and senior officials	3,368	7.9	4.6	2.8	15.3
Professional occupations	2,968	11.9	6.9	5.5	24.3
Associate professional and technical	3,264	10.9	7.9	4.8	23.6
Administrative and secretarial	3,218	7.4	4.8	2.1	14.3
Skilled trades	2,029	3.9	3.1	3.4	10.4
Personal service occupations	1,875	8.4	8.5	6.2	23.2
Sales and customer service occupations	2,095	7.1	4.7	1.3	13.2
Process, plant and machine operatives	1,775	2.5	3.7	1.0	7.2
Elementary occupations	2,905	5.3	3.0	1.1	9.4
By full-time/part-time work[e]					
Full-time	17,635	7.1	5.6	3.4	16.1
Part-time	5,868	9.3	4.3	2.6	16.1
of which:					
students	1,149	21.7	2.6	3.9	28.1
could not find full-time job	459	4.7	3.7	2.5	10.9
did not want full-time job	4,099	6.5	4.9	2.3	13.7
ill or disability	137	4.1	2.6	1.3	8.0
By employment status					
Permanent	22,193	7.5	5.3	3.2	15.9
Temporary	1,309	10.3	5.9	3.3	19.6
of which					
seasonal/casual work	318	11.7	3.7	–	17.3
contract for fixed term or task	630	11.0	7.4	3.8	22.3
agency temping	221	6.9	4.8	–	12.8
other	140	9.4	–	7.9	23.2

a Job-related training includes both on- and off-the-job training.
b Employees are those in employment excluding the self-employed, unpaid family workers and those on government employment and training programmes.
c Expressed as a percentage of the total number of people in each group.
d Apart from rounding, figures may not sum to grand totals because of questions in the LFS which were unanswered or did not apply.
e The split between employees working full-time and part-time is based on respondents' own assessment.

Source: DfES, 2004b

Table 90: **Participation in job-related training[a] in the previous four weeks, by economic activity and age, United Kingdom, 2004**

	All	Males	Females	All	Males	Females
	(Thousands)			(%)[b]		
All people						
All	5,112	2,330	2,781	14.1	12.5	15.8
16–19	664	348	316	21.8	22.4	21.2
20–24	823	386	437	22.8	22.4	21.2
25–29	595	261	334	16.8	15.1	18.4
30–39	1,245	563	682	14.2	13.1	15.2
40–49	1,071	432	639	12.9	10.5	15.2
50–64	714	341	373	7.9	6.6	9.8
Employees[c]						
All	3,791	1,699	2,092	16.1	14.0	18.4
16–19	318	168	150	22.6	24.4	20.9
20–24	482	221	262	20.5	18.3	22.8
25–29	471	207	264	18.3	15.7	21.0
30–39	1,020	476	544	16.4	14.8	18.2
40–49	900	356	544	15.4	12.2	18.5
50–64	600	272	329	11.7	9.7	14.2
Self-employed						
All	248	146	102	7.5	5.9	12.0
16–19	–	–	–	–	–	–
20–24	13	–	–	10.8	–	–
25–29	19	12	–	9.3	7.5	–
30–39	71	34	37	8.3	5.6	14.7
40–49	76	47	29	7.8	6.8	10.5
50–64	64	43	22	5.7	4.8	9.0
ILO unemployed						
All	139	73	67	10.4	9.4	11.8
16–19	46	27	19	16.9	17.0	16.6
20–24	27	13	14	12.6	11.3	14.3
25–29	–	–	–	–	–	–
30–39	25	14	11	8.9	8.7	9.0
40–49	19	–	12	8.8	–	11.3
50–64	12	–	–	6.2	–	–
Economically inactive[d]						
All	846	365	481	10.7	11.6	10.1
16–19	252	121	131	19.8	18.9	20.6
20–24	285	136	148	31.9	38.5	27.5
25–29	90	35	55	15.1	22.1	12.6
30–39	120	36	84	8.5	11.8	7.6
40–49	68	19	49	5.5	5.1	5.7
50–64	31	18	13	1.2	1.3	1.1

a Job-related training includes both on- and off-the-job training.
b Expressed as a percentage of the total number of people in each group.
c Employees are those in employment excluding self-employed, unpaid family workers and those on government employment and training programmes.
d Economically inactive are those who are neither in employment nor ILO unemployed.

Source: DfES, 2004b

Table 91: **Participation in job-related training,[a] by employees[b] in the previous four weeks, by type of training and a range of personal characteristics, United Kingdom, Spring 2004**

	Total number of employees	of which: receiving off-the-job training[c]	receiving on-the-job training	receiving both on- and off-the-job training	receiving any training
	(Thousands)	(%)[c]	(%)	(%)	(%)
All employees	23,510	7.7	5.3	3.2	16.1
By sex					
Males	12,144	6.6	4.7	2.7	14.0
Females	11,365	8.8	5.9	3.7	18.4
By age					
16–19	1,406	9.9	6.6	6.1	22.6
20–24	2,357	9.6	6.4	4.5	20.5
25–29	2,570	8.3	6.1	3.9	18.3
30–39	6,207	7.9	5.2	3.4	16.4
40–49	5,845	7.4	5.3	2.7	15.4
50–64	5,125	5.9	4.1	1.6	11.7
By ethnic origin					
White	21,856	7.6	5.2	3.2	16.0
Non-white	1,653	7.8	6.2	3.3	17.3
of which:					
mixed	147	9.3	8.7	–	22.4
Asian or Asian British	774	6.4	5.1	2.6	14.1
black or black British	453	8.5	7.3	4.1	19.9
Chinese	73	–	–	–	16.5
other ethnic group	199	9.2	7.3	3.3	19.7
By highest qualification held					
Degree or equivalent	4,829	11.9	6.3	4.4	22.6
Higher education qualification (below degree level)	2,393	12.0	6.9	4.7	23.6
GCE A-Level or equivalent	5,690	7.7	5.1	3.2	16.0
GCSE grades A* to C or equivalent	5,236	6.0	5.3	2.9	14.2
Other	3,018	4.9	4.8	2.1	11.8
None	2,217	1.5	2.7	1.0	5.1
By region					
United Kingdom	23,510	7.7	5.3	3.2	16.1
North East	952	8.5	6.3	4.3	19.2
North West	2,642	7.5	5.6	2.8	16.0
Yorkshire and the Humber	2,000	7.6	5.5	3.3	16.5
East Midlands	1,747	7.3	5.9	3.8	17.0
West Midlands	2,090	7.2	4.8	3.3	15.3
East	2,241	7.1	4.2	3.1	14.5
London	2,821	7.9	5.3	3.1	16.3
South East	3,284	7.7	5.6	3.2	16.5
South West	1,957	7.9	5.2	3.0	16.1
England	19,734	7.6	5.3	3.2	16.2
Wales	1,113	8.7	5.8	3.6	18.2
Scotland	2,085	8.0	5.3	2.9	16.2
Northern Ireland	577	6.2	2.9	–	10.6

a Job-related training includes both on- and off-the-job training.
b Employees are those in employment excluding self-employed, unpaid family workers and those on government employment and training programmes.
c Expressed as a percentage of the total number of people in each group.

Source: DfES, 2004b

6.11 Age and job-related training

Despite the ageing of the workforce, one of the persistent characteristics of job-related training is the extent to which it declines with the age of employees. Scottish data illustrate this trend, showing that those aged 16–24 are twice as likely as those aged 55+ to receive job-related training (Table 92).

Figure 50, based on an Institute for Employment Studies analysis of the Labour Force Survey, spring 2004, also illustrates the sharp decline in training participation and training offers for workers aged over 50.

Table 92: **Working-age[a] people in employment receiving job-related training in the previous three months, Scotland, 2004**

	(Thousands)	(%)
All in employment	672	30.8
Age band		
16–24	100	38.2
25–34	166	34.3
35–44	205	32.1
45–54	150	28.0
55–59/64	51	19.4
Male	335	28.7
Female	338	33.2
White	662	30.9
Non-white	10	26.9

Levels are rounded to the nearest thousand.
Totals may not equal the sum of individual components due to rounding.
a Working age is defined as 16–59 for females and 16–64 for males.

Source: Scottish Executive, 2004

Figure 50: **Employees offered and/or receiving education or training in the previous 13 weeks, by age, Great Britain, 2004**

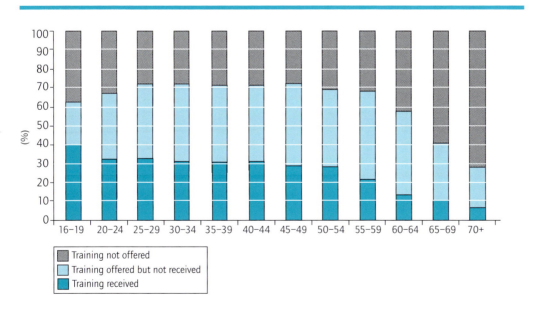

Source: Newton *et al*, 2005

Table 93: **Duration of training period (those engaged in training in the previous four weeks only), Great Britain, 2004**

Age	16–19	20–24	25–29	30–34	35–39	40–44	45–49	50–54	55–59	60–64
					(%)					
Duration										
Less than 6 months	14.7	32.2	48.4	55.4	56.5	59.5	61.5	66.1	68.9	71.8
6 months, less than 1 year	6.8	6.2	4.5	6.0	6.0	6.3	5.2	5.0	–	–
1 year, less than 2 years	16.8	10.7	9.2	6.9	7.5	6.7	6.1	4.3	5.1	–
2 years or more	49.3	33.6	18.0	14.0	10.5	8.6	8.5	5.4	–	–
Ongoing/no definite limit	12.4	17.4	19.9	17.7	19.5	18.9	18.7	19.2	18.3	21.4
Number (thousands)	280	420	418	448	497	443	387	334	209	55

Source: Newton *et al*, 2004

Newton *et al*'s analysis found a clear association between age and the amount and length of training offered to and received by workers. Older workers were more likely only to have received on-the-job training, and any off-the-job training received tends to be of very short duration (Table 93).

6.12 Sex differences in job-related training

Table 94 and Figure 51 illustrate that across each age cohort, female employees are more likely to have received training in the last 13 weeks than male workers.

Figure 51: **Employees receiving job-related training in the previous four weeks, by sex and age, United Kingdom, 2004**

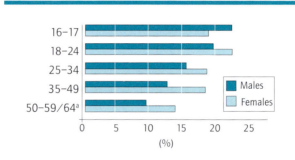

a Males aged 50–64, females aged 50–59.

Source: DfES and Skills from the Labour Force Survey

Table 94: **Workers receiving training in the previous 13 weeks, by sex and age, Great Britain, 2004**

Age	16–24	25–34	35–44	45–54	55–59	60–64	65+
				(%)[a]			
Male	34.6	31.1	27.5	26.8	20.7	11.9	6.9
Female	37.3	35.9	34.6	32.6	25.3	18.3	11.5
All cases	35.9	33.4	31.0	29.8	23.0	14.6	9.0

a Expressed as a percentage of total people in age group.

Source: Newton *et al*, 2004

As seen in the previous sections, there is a strong tendency for women and men to follow different and stereotypical areas of learning. This pattern is reflected in work-related training. Table 95 clearly illustrates this trend, showing that women predominate in apprenticeships training in early years care and education, hairdressing, travel, health and social care (all lower paid occupational areas), while men predominate in apprenticeships in electrotechnical, plumbing, motor industry, construction and engineering occupational areas.

The pattern remained unchanged in the following year. In 2003–04, women held 91 per cent of apprenticeships in health & social care but only 3 per cent of apprenticeships in engineering and 1 per cent in construction, where men are concentrated. So even though women (particularly young women) are now out-performing young men in education, their choice of subject is inevitably affecting their employment patterns and earnings potential.

Different motivations, as well as social custom, underlie these choices.

6.13 Vocational course choice: sex differences

Analysis of calls to the learndirect learning advice line during 2004 showed that male callers cite financial rewards as their key motivation for training, whereas female callers cite job satisfaction and the prospect of doing something socially worthwhile as their prime motivation.

Men were also motivated by the prospect of eventual self-employment and the appeal of working with their hands on practical tasks. The analysis confirms Table 95 in showing that there has been a shift from interest in IT professions – a strong interest 4–5 years ago – to an interest in skilled trades. It identified a 'massive trend' for men to want to train for industries that offer relatively high rates of pay due to current skills shortages. The four most popular areas of training requested by men during 2004 were:

- Plumbing

Table 95: **Workers receiving training in the previous 13 weeks, by sex and age, Great Britain, 2004**

Selected sectors	Women		Men	
	AMAs[a]	FMAs[a]	AMAs	FMAs
	(%)			
Early years care & education	97.5	97.0	2.5	3.0
Hairdressing	92.8	92.3	7.2	7.7
Travel services	89.9	82.5	10.1	17.5
Health & social care	87.7	90.0	12.3	10.0
Business administration	81.1	76.1	18.9	23.9
Customer service	68.4	67.9	31.6	32.1
Retail	64.2	67.4	35.8	32.6
Accountancy	63.1	63.6	36.9	36.4
Hospitality	49.0	52.1	51.0	47.9
Sports & recreation	39.7	37.1	60.3	62.9
IT & electronic services	13.2	17.2	86.8	82.8
Engineering	3.1	6.0	96.9	94.0
Construction	1.9	0.7	98.1	99.3
Motor industry	1.4	1.4	98.6	98.6
Plumbing	0.6	0.7	99.4	99.3
Electrotechnical	0.4	1.0	99.6	99.0
All sectors[b]	41.4	53.0	58.6	47.0

a AMA/FMA=Advanced/Foundation Modern Apprenticeship.
b Including those not shown separately.

Source: LSC, 2004b

- Electrical installation,
- Plastering,
- Construction – general.

Men were also interested in courses in literacy, language and numeracy.

For women, the most popular areas of training asked about by women in 2004 were
- Childcare/Nursery nursing,
- Nursing/midwifery,
- Teaching,
- Beauty therapy/Hairdressing,
- Classroom Assistant courses.

Younger women were more interested than older ones in beauty therapy/hairdressing and administration. Classroom assistant courses were more popular among older women – usually women returners with children.

The most popular area sought by people over 55 was computer literacy. Teaching and counselling courses were also popular with the older age group. (Learndirect, 2004).

6.14 Employer Training Pilots (ETP)[14]

ETP is a government initiative to increase work-related training.

In 2003–04, over 14,000 companies and 100,000 learners registered in ETP and almost 23,000 employers in England had taken part altogether by 2004.

An evaluation of the pilot scheme showed that 70 per cent of the companies taking part employ less than 250 people and a quarter, fewer than ten.

Of the 95 per cent of learners who have stayed in the training 10.2 per cent are from the black and Asian communities and 55.7 per cent are female (DfES, 2004c).

6.15 Training for unemployed people

Jobcentre Plus provision

Jobcentre Plus provision includes provision for improving adult literacy, language and numeracy skills (Skills for Life) for groups such as:
- unemployed people and benefit recipients,
- young adults in the workforce and those in low skilled jobs,
- parents,
- prisoners and probationers,
- groups at high risk of social exclusion.

Jobseeker's Allowance (JSA) recipients are required to declare part-time participation and a decision is then made as to whether a course can be treated as being 'part time' (less than 16 hours).

Employment programmes include:
- The mandatory New Deals and Work Based

Learning for Adults (WBLA) for people receiving the job-seeker's allowance. Training is offered through:
- Basic Employability Training (BET) – Targeted at individuals with the lowest skills levels This training offers a mix of basic skills, wider soft skills and work experience. Basic Employability Training is offered in WBLA and is voluntary, full time and lasts for up to 26 weeks.
- Full-Time Education and Training (FTET) – Available as a New Deal for Young People, 18–24 (mandatory programme) option;
- Basic Employability Training in New Deal 25 plus (a mandatory programme) – designed mainly for clients who would normally be below entry Level 3.
- ESOL (English for Speakers of Other Languages) – Offered in BET and FTET
- Short Intensive Basic Skills, full-time courses (SIBS) – Designed for those with better skills but still below Level 1.

Section 7

Quality issues in provision for adults

7.1 Best providers of learning for adults

According to the Report of the Chief Inspector 2003–04 (ALI, 2004) 17 per cent of the total 470 initial inspections conducted in England by the ALI were 'top providers' (i.e. judged good or outstanding in every area of their activities), compared with 13 per cent in the previous year. (NB no specialist colleges of dance, drama and the arts were inspected in 2003–04.)

The Inspectorate found that fourteen of the best providers in 2003–04 (41 per cent) were in the North of England and 10 (30 per cent) in the South (a change from 2002–03 when most of those considered best were in the South).

The majority of those judged to be the best providers were those involved in work-based learning. Only four adult and community learning providers were included, two of these being charities, one a specialist adult college and only one a local authority, despite the fact that, according to the Chief Inspector, ' the heartland of adult and community learning lies in local authorities' (Table 96).

Twenty-one further education colleges were among the best providers. Eleven of these were sixth form colleges, offering varying proportions of part-time provision for adults; three were general further education/tertiary colleges or specialist vocational colleges; three were residential colleges for people with learning difficulties or disabilities; and the remaining four were higher education institutions with substantial further education.

Table 96: **Best providers according to Adult Learning Inspectorate inspections, England, 2003–04**

• Work-based learning (LSC-funded)	34
• Jobcentre Plus programmes	17
• Adult and community learning	4
• Learndirect hubs	1
• General further education, tertiary and land-based vocational colleges	2
• Sixth form colleges	11
• Higher education institutions	4
• Specialist colleges for people with learning difficulties or disabilities	3

Source: Adult Learning Inspectorate, 2004

The higher education institutions comprised three art and design colleges and the Birmingham College of Food, Tourism and Creative Studies, the only college to achieve grade 1 across the board.

Among general further education/ tertiary colleges, only Brockenhurst College in Hampshire and South Cheshire College were among those considered top providers.

The chief Inspector describes as disappointing the lack of top providers offering information & communications technology (ICT) and the relatively few top providers specialising in construction.

Thirteen (38 per cent) of the top work-based learning providers were commercial training companies. Two work-based learning providers achieved grade 1 for every aspect of their provision

– BMW (GB) Limited and Sandwell and West Birmingham Hospitals NHS Trust.

Among the 34 top work-based learning providers, seven (16 per cent) specialised in care, six (14 per cent) in foundation studies including basic skills and five (12 per cent) in business administration.

Most of the best work-based provision was found to be in small providers (65 per cent have fewer than 100 learners), with a single area of learning (79 per cent).

The Chief Inspector noted a marked improvement in Jobcentre Plus provision (the New Deals, Ambitions and other specialist programmes for unemployed people). The best Jobcentre Plus provider of 2003–04, Positive People Development, was awarded grade 1 across the board, was much larger than the average, with over 400 learners

Table 97: **Top providers, England, 2003–04**

1st Choice Training	Franklin College	Richard Huish College
Accounting Technician Training Services Ltd	G B Transport Training Services Limited	Royal Mail Group
Andrew Collinge	Greenhead College	Royal School for the Deaf
Aquinas College	Humberside Engineering Training Association Limited	RWE Innogy plc
Arts Institute at Bournemouth	HMP Foston Hall	Salford and Trafford Engineering Group Training Association (STEGTA) Limited
B L Hairdressing Training	Hoskins Management Development Limited	Sandwell and West Birmingham Hospitals NHS Trust
Barnsley MBC	InBiz	Sandwell Council of Voluntary Organisations
Birmingham College of Food, Tourism & Creative Studies	Into Business Scheme	Sir John Deane's College
BMW (GB) Limited	Islington CAB (CABCOM)	Slough Borough Council
BOSCO Centre	John Clive Training	South Cheshire College
Brighton and Hove City Council (Workstep)	JTL	Sparsholt College, Hampshire
British Gas (British Gas Engineering Academy)	King Edward VI College, Stourbridge	Springboard
Brockenhurst College	Lifetime Health and Fitness	Stockton-on-Tees LEA
Business Enterprise Support Ltd	Mercia Partnership (UK) Ltd	Support Into Work
Camelot Courier Training Ltd	Minstead Training Project	Sutton & District Training Limited
Careconnect Learning Limited	Newcastle NHS Trust	Taxi Trade Promotions Limited
Cheltenham Community Project	Northamptonshire County Council	Tees and North East Yorkshire NHS Trust
College of Richard Collyer in Horsham	Notre Dame Sixth Form College	The London Institute
Cumbria Institute of the Arts	Oldham Sixth Form College	Triangle Training Ltd
Derwent Training Association	Open Door Adult Learning Centre	TTE Management & Technical Training
Didac Limited	Orange plc	Warrington Borough Council
Direct Training Ltd	Partners For Business	West Anglia Training Association
Dorton College	Partnership for Learning	Westwind Air Bearings Ltd
East Riding Training Services	Pendleton College	Workability (Impact Initiatives)
Energy and Utility Skills Limited	Positive People Development	Working Men's College
Fast Lane Training Services	Pre-School Learning Alliance	
	Queen Elizabeth Sixth Form College	

Source: Adult Learning Inspectorate, 2004

7.2 Characteristics of good learning provision

The main characteristics of good adult learning provision are described by the Chief Inspector as 'remarkably consistent' across the range of providers. These are:
● High rates of retention, achievement or progression to employment.
● Good teaching, training and skills development
● Good resources for learning.
● Good management, notably in using data to illuminate quality issues and in guaranteeing equality of opportunity for learners.

These characteristics were 'underpinned by sound practice in recruiting, selecting, initially assessing and inducting learners; assessment and verification; key skills teaching and assessment; jobsearch; staff development and business planning'. (ALI, 2004)

7.3 Poor providers in 2003–04

The proportion of providers judged to be poor fell from 14 per cent in 2002–03 to 10 per cent. The greatest improvement was seen in LSC-funded work-based learning.

The weakest providers were national organisations, many of which were in the Midlands.

Forty-seven providers were awarded grade 4 or 5 for every aspect of their provision in 2003–04. Table 98 shows the list of providers considered poor.

Among work-based learning providers, eight of the 26 considered poor were commercial training organisations, and 10, employers or employers' group training associations. Among the rest, four were charities and four local authorities.

Eleven of the 18 (61 per cent) poor providers of Jobcentre Plus programmes were local authorities, five (28 per cent) were commercial providers and the remaining two, charities.

The weakest provision appeared to be in the North of England, where unemployment is highest

Independent specialist colleges for people with learning difficulties and/or disabilities had proportionately more unsatisfactory provision than general further education colleges.

Table 98: **Poor providers, England, 2003–04**

Adecco UK Ltd	Devonport Royal Dockyard Limited	North Tyneside Metropolitan Borough Council
Aspin House College	Doncaster Rotherham & District Motor Trades GTA Ltd	Northumberland County Council
Birmingham Hotel & Catering Academy	eTraining	Nottingham City Council (Workstep)
Business Network Ltd	First 4 Fitness	Poole Borough Council[a]
Calderdale MBC (Workstep)	Focus Vision Limited	South Tyneside Metropolitan Borough Council (Workstep)
Camden ITEC	Future Strategies Consulting Ltd	Suffolk County Council Gold
Citizen 2000	GeTaHead Training	The Academy – Professional Hairdressing Education
City of Sunderland Workline[a]	Greenwich School of Management	The Bridge
CLG (Great Britain) Ltd	Groundwork Thames Gateway London South	The Engineering Hub
Client Support and Research Unit	Hartley Centre (Church Army)	The Laird Foundation
Cobden Training Services	Humber Client/Contractor Training Association	The Royal Wolverhampton Hospitals NHS Trust
Community Network Training	Inner London Training Limited	Trafford MBC (Workstep)[a]
Community Solutions Limited	Jewson Limited	Trent Park Equestrian Centre
Corporate Training and Development	Leicestershire County Council (Workstep)	
Corporate Vocational Training	MBW Training Services	
County Training (Gloucestershire)	Middlesbrough Borough Council	
Crowns Worthing Limited		
Derby Business College Limited		

a Awarded grade 5 for every aspect of provision.

Source: ALI, 2004

The list of poorest providers included one provider of adult and community learning and one learndirect hub, a national industry-sector organisation.

7.4 Weakest areas of learning

In work-based provision, business administration, retailing and customer service accounted for nearly half of the areas of learning judged as weakest. Serious problems were also noted in provision for construction with success rates among construction apprentices described as 'often appalling'.

Among the 18 poor Jobcentre Plus providers, ten offered Workstep (for adults with disabilities or learning difficulties). All the worst providers of Workstep were local authorities, three of which were awarded grade 5 for every aspect of their provision (Table 98).

The Chief Inspector describes as 'intolerable' that vulnerable adults with disabilities or learning difficulties should be the most likely to receive a bad learning experience and calls for the improvement of Workstep as a priority.

The Chief Inspector comments on the mediocre performance of many providers in delivering foundation studies in 2003–04. This was among the weakest areas of learning in colleges. Real improvements in foundation studies were seen mostly in adult and community learning, notably in family learning and community development, and in prisons, where the proportion of good or outstanding grades nearly doubled from 22 to 42 per cent.

7.5 Areas of concern

The Chief Inspector notes that although many providers, especially local education authorities, had better strategic planning, as well as a stronger focus on increasing participation and working in partnership, 60 per cent of adult and community learning providers were weak in the area of quality assurance. He was particularly concerned at the low

standards of provision for people with learning difficulties or disabilities; those who have failed, or who have been failed, at school, and offenders

The inspections also showed that the curriculum was often poorly planned and managed and that few providers based their programmes on local needs. Providers were also slow to change their traditional offering and progression routes were seldom clearly marked. Many learners had no formal assessment of their skills and knowledge at the beginning of a course and providers had scant information with which to shape a useful learning plan and set targets.

In addition, part-time tutors were not given enough support. While a few providers invested time and money in venues and equipment, too many ran courses in sub-standard accommodation and relied on tutors or learners to bring equipment.

7.6 Characteristics of the poorest providers

The Inspectorate found the characteristics of the poorest providers to be:
- weak quality management, including use of data and self-assessment,
- little protection of equality of opportunity,
- low rates of retention, achievement or progression to employment,
- weak assessment of needs and support for disadvantaged learners,
- poor management, including control of subcontractors.

7.7 Inspectorate findings for different types of provider

Adult and community learning
Many family learning and community development programmes were very successful and teaching was judged as good.

The best-taught subjects were art & design, health and care, and family learning.

Most of the unsatisfactory teaching and learning was in languages, sport and leisure, and foundation programmes.

The Chief Inspector noted that industrial changes have been reflected in adult and vocational learning provision, with new areas of the curriculum well developed such as recreational use of the countryside, horticulture and garden design.

Sciences and mathematics, and visual and performing arts and media courses, were particularly successful at arranging a wide range of enrichment activities to enthuse learners.

Neither languages nor sports and fitness received good inspection grades. It was felt that too many native speakers are being employed who do not have a good grasp of interactive and innovative teaching methods, and that there is an over-dependence on the use of English rather than the target language in the classroom.

In sport and fitness, the major concern was health and safety awareness, poor initial assessment and problems with accommodation, particularly where premises are used for many purposes.

In his annual report for 2004 the Chief Inspector refers to a 'conspiracy of niceness' in which the shortcomings of part-time tutors who have taught, unsupervised, for many years are ignored or condoned. He also comments that poor provision is characterised by 'randomness'.

Colleges

Most colleges were working towards widening participation from all sections of the community, working increasingly collaboratively and encouraging learners to progress from further to higher education.

Teaching and learning for adults was considered better than for young people aged 16 to 19. The best teaching was seen in visual and performing arts and media, and in hospitality lessons; the poorest in construction and in retailing and customer service.

Success and retention rates were higher for full-time learners than those studying part time.

Support was not always readily available for people studying part time or in the evenings. Initial guidance and assessment were weak in many colleges.

Few colleges responded successfully to meeting employer needs or gave sufficient priority to work-based learning.

Many colleges did not have enough appropriately experienced and qualified teachers to help learners develop their literacy, numeracy and language skills.

Learndirect

The Inspectorate found that good leadership and management at hub level resulted in steady improvements in quality during a period of major change. Inspection grades improved since 2002–03, although the vast majority of provision was no more than satisfactory.

Rates of retention and achievement had improved and management information was being used more productively to set and monitor targets.

Quality assurance processes were ineffectively applied by many hubs. There was a tendency to focus on audit and compliance rather than quality improvement.

Learndirect hubs were successfully attracting learners from under-represented groups although learning centres did not have enough staff qualified to teach and support learners who needed help with literacy, numeracy or language development. Monitoring of learners' progress on 'skills for life' courses was weak.

Prisons

Teaching and learning were found to be good in most areas of learning. Many learners developed good practical skills essential to their chosen vocational area. The best areas were business industrial cleaning, construction and engineering. Resources for training had improved.

However, foundation programmes were poor. About one in five prisons had unsatisfactory provision for literacy, numeracy and language support, and for people with specific learning difficulties, such as dyslexia.

Planning to meet individual learners needs was considered inadequate. Many prisoners were not allocated to the most appropriate type of training and few prisons knew how many prisoners had literacy, numeracy or language problems.

The range of programmes was found to be too narrow and did not meet the needs of the prison population. By targeting learners at Levels 1 and 2, prisons did not give sufficient opportunities to prisoners who would benefit from other levels of programme, whether higher or lower. The range of subjects was also considered too narrow.

Co-ordination of education or training between prisons was very poor. Records and information were not passed on. In many prisons, communication between the education department and other training areas was poor. Not enough was done to ensure that prisoners were in a good position to gain employment on their release.

Over 80 per cent of prisons were awarded unsatisfactory or worse grades for quality assurance.

Work-based learning

Grades given for work-based learning have risen since 2002–03 and most learning sessions were well managed and professionally delivered. The highest proportion of good teaching was in hospitality, with foundation programmes providing the largest proportion of poor teaching.

However, quality assurance was still unsatisfactory in nearly half the providers inspected. Engineering performed particularly well in terms of good grades. Hospitality, sport, leisure and travel was the poorest area of learning, with over 60 per cent deemed inadequate.

Less than a third of all modern apprentices completed the full requirements of their apprenticeship framework.

Support for the development of learners' literacy, numeracy and language skills was inadequate. Staff providing the support rarely had appropriate qualifications and expertise.

Few providers evaluated the quality of their training effectively. Quality assurance arrangements were often insufficiently rigorous in assessing the quality of on-the-job learning, progress reviews and initial assessment.

7.8 Learner satisfaction

The national Learner Satisfaction Survey: conducted for the LSC in 2003–04 found that:
- Over 90 per cent of FE learners were 'fairly', 'very' or 'extremely' satisfied with their overall learning experience.
- 72 per cent of learners in FE delivered by adult learning providers are very or extremely satisfied and 80 per cent of those on non-accredited ACL courses are very or extremely satisfied.
- 60 per cent of FE learners said they were 'very' likely to return to learning within the next 3 years (LSC, 2004b).

References

Aldridge, F and Tuckett, A (2005) *Better news this time? The NIACE Survey on Adult Participation in Learning 2005*, Leicester: NIACE.

ALI (Adult Learning Inspectorate) (2004) *Annual Report of the Chief Inspector 2003–04*, Nottingham: ALI.

ALI (Adult Learning Inspectorate) and Ofsted (2003) *Literacy, numeracy and English for speakers of other languages: a survey of current practice in post-16 and adult provision*, Nottingham: ALI.

Babb, P, Martin, J and Haezewindt, P (eds) (2004) *Focus on Social Inequalities* 2004 Edition, Newport: Office for National Statistics.

Baty, P (2005) 'Visa crisis harms UK, Blair told', *The Times Higher Education Supplement*, March 11, p 2.

Blanden, J, Gregg, P and Machin, S (2005) *Intergenerational Mobility in Europe and North America*, London: Centre for Economic Performance.

Campbell, A (2005) '2 million working from home', *Metro*, February 11.

Centre for Economic Performance (2004) *Skills Audit Update*, London: LSE Centre for Economic Performance.

CIPD (Chartered Institute of Personnel and Development) (2004) *Recruitment, Retention and Turnover 2004: a survey of the UK and Ireland*, (Citizens Online, 2005) http://www.children-go-online.net/

DfES (Department for Education and Skills) (2003a) *21st Century Skills: Realising our Potential*, Nottingham: DfES.

DfES (Department for Education and Skills) (2003b) *The Skills for Life Survey: A National Needs and Impact Survey of Literacy, Numeracy and ICT Skills*, Nottingham: DfES.

DfES (Department for Education and Skills) (2004a) *The level of highest qualification held by young people and adults: England 2003: Statistical First Release* 03/2004, 5 February 2004, Nottingham: DfES.

DfES (Department for Education and Skills) (2004b) *Statistics of Education: Education and Training Statistics for the United Kingdom*, 2004 edition, Nottingham: DfES.

DfES (Department for Education and Skills) (2004c) *Skills for Life: Annual Review 2003–2004: progress in raising standards in provision and learners' achievements*, Nottingham: DfES.

DfES (Department for Education and Skills) (2004d) *GCE/VCE A/AS Results for Young People in England, 2003/04 (Provisional): Statistical First Release* 38/2004, 21 October 2004, Nottingham: DfES.

DfES (Department for Education and Skills) (2005a) *Skills: Getting On In Business, Getting On At Work* (White Paper), DfES/Stationery Office.

DfES (Department for Education and Skills) (2005b) *GCSE and Equivalent Results and Associated Value Added Measures for Young People in England 2003/04 (Revised): Statistical First Release* 01/2005, 12 January 2005, Nottingham: DfES.

DfES (Department for Education and Skills) (2005c) *GCE/VCE A/AS Results in England, 2003/04 (Revised): Statistical First Release* 02/2005, 12 January 2005, Nottingham: DfES.

DfES (Department for Education and Skills) (2005d) *GCE/VCE A/AS Examination Results for Young People in England 2003/2004 (Final): Statistical First Release* 26/2005, 30 June 2005, Nottingham: DfES.

DfES (Department for Education and Skills) (2005e) Learning and Skills Council Documents: *Learner Numbers*, available at: http://www.lsc.gov.uk/National/Partners/Data/Statistics/LearnerStatistics/LearnerNumbers/Default.htm

DfES (Department for Education and Skills) (2005f) *Participation in education, training and employment by 16-18 year olds in England: 1985 to 2003 (Revised): Statistical First Release* 03/2005, 27 January 2005, Nottingham: DfES.

Dodd, T, Sian, S, Povey, D and Walker, A (2004) *Crime in England and Wales 2003/2004*, London: Home Office

DTI (Department of Trade and Industry) (2004) *Interim update of key indicators of women's position in Britain*, London: Department of Trade and Industry.

DWP (Department of Work and Pensions) (2005a) *Opportunity Age: Meeting the challenges of ageing in the 21st century*, London: Department of Work and Pensions.

DWP (Department of Work and Pensions) (2005b) *First Release Client Group Analysis: Quarterly Bulletin on the*

Population of Working Age on Key Benefits – November 2004, 1IAD160305-QBWA-Mar05, Newcastle-upon-Tyne: DWP.

EOC (Equal Opportunities Commission) (2005), *Facts about Women and Men in Great Britain 2005*, London: EOC.

Grattan, P (2005) 'Employment and age', *Working Brief*, 164, p 14, London: Centre for Social and Economic Inclusion.

Griffiths Commission on Personal Debt (2005) *What price credit?* London: Centre for Social Justice.

HESA (Higher Education Statistics Agency) (2004a), *Statistical overview of higher education: HE statistics for the United Kingdom 2002/03* (press release 79), Cheltenham: HESA.

HESA (Higher Education Statistics Agency) (2004b), *Destinations of leavers from higher education in the United Kingdom for the academic year 2002/03*, SFR 77, Cheltenham: HESA.

HESA (Higher Education Statistics Agency) (2005a) *Students in HEIs 2003/2004*, Reference Volume, Cheltenham: HESA.

HESA (Higher Education Statistics Agency) (2005b) *Part-time first-years up by 4.2 per cent* (PR 86), Cheltenham: HESA.

HESA (Higher Education Statistics Agency) (2005c) *First year he student numbers exceed one million mark* (PR 83), Cheltenham: HESA.

HESA (Higher Education Statistics Agency) (2005d) *Qualifications obtained by and examination results of HE students and HEIs in United Kingdom for academic year 2003–04*, SFR 82, Cheltenham: HESA.

Hogarth, T, Shury, J, Vivian, D, Wilson, R and Winterbotham, M (2004) *National employers' skills survey 2003: Main report*, Coventry: Learning and Skills Council.

Home Office (2003) *Citizenship Survey: People, Families and Communities*, London: Home Office.

Home Office (2004) *Statistical Bulletin 2004: Asylum Statistics*, United Kingdom 2003, second edition, London: Home Office.

Humphries, C (2005) 'Skills in a Global Economy', address at Worldskills Leaders Forum, 25 May 2005, Helsinki.

Learndirect (2004) *Facts and Figures*, 10 January, Sheffield: learndirect.

Local Area Labour Force Surveys – see ONS.

LSC (Learning and Skills Council) (2004a) *The Skills we need: Our annual statement of priorities*, Coventry: LSC.

LSC (Learning and Skills Council) (2004b) *National Learner Satisfaction Survey: Adult and Community learning Providers Summary Report 2002–03*, Coventry: LSC.

LSC (Learning and Skills Council) (2004c) *Equality and Diversity Report*, Coventry: LSC.

LSC (Learning and Skills Council) (2004d) *Further education, work-based learning for young people and adult and community learning – learner numbers in England: 2003/2004* [Prepared and published by the Learning and Skills Council in consultation with DfES statisticians]: ILR/SFR05/2004, 14 December 2004, Coventry: LSC.

LSC (Learning and Skills Council) (2005a) *Skills in England: 2004*, Vol. 1, Coventry: LSC.

LSC (Learning and Skills Council) (2005b) *Further education, work-based learning for young people and adult and community learning – learner numbers in England* ILR/SFR06/2005, 22 March 2005, Coventry: LSC.

LSC (Learning and Skills Council) (2005c) *Further education and work based learning for young people – learner outcomes in England*: ILR/SFR07/2005, 28 June 2005, Coventry: LSC.

LSC (Learning and Skills Council) (2005d) Documents: *Learner Numbers*, available at: http://www.lsc.gov.uk/National/Partners/Data/Statistics/LearnerStatistics/LearnerNumbers/Default.htm

NAO (National Audit Office) and Department for Education and Skills (2004) *Skills for life: Improving adult literacy and numeracy: report by the Comptroller and Auditor General*, Stationery Office. London.

National Assembly for Wales (2005) *Key Education Statistics Wales 2004*, Cardiff: Education Training and Economic Statistics Unit.

New Policy Institute (2005) *Monitoring poverty and social exclusion 2004*, a report for the Joseph Rowntree Foundation, London: NPI.

Newton, B, Hurstfield, J, Miller, L, Bates, P (2005) *Training a Mixed-Age Workforce: Practical Tips and Guidance For Extending Working Lives*, Falmer: Institute for Employment Studies.

NIACE (2005) *Fees survey 2003–04; Indicators of fee levels charged to part-time adult students by Local Education Authorities and Colleges*, Leicester: NIACE.

OECD (Organisation for Economic Cooperation and Development) (2004a) *Education at a Glance*, Paris: OECD.

OECD (Organisation for Economic Cooperation and Development) (2004b) *Thematic review on adult learning*, United Kingdom (England), Paris: OECD.

ONS (Office of National Statistics) (2005a) *Social Trends 35*, London: ONS.

ONS (Office of National Statistics) *Annual Local Area Labour Force Surveys* and 2003–04 *Summary Publication*.

Royal Society (2005) *Science, engineering & technology and the UK's ethnic minority population*, London: Royal Society.

Schuller, T (2005) 'Demographic challenges: family structures and ageing', in Tuckett, A and McAulay, A (eds) *Demography and Older Learners: Approaches to a new policy challenge*, Leicester: NIACE.

Scottish Executive (2003) *Statistics Online: Scotland's People: Results from the 2003 Scottish Household Survey Annual*, Edinburgh: Scottish Executive.

Scottish Executive (2004) *Annual Scottish Labour Force Survey 2003–04*, Edinburgh: Scottish Executive.

Scottish Executive (2005) *Students in higher education in Scotland 2003–04*, Edinburgh: Scottish Executive.

TAEN (Third Age Employment Network) (2005a) Newsletter, Summer Issue, London: TAEN.

TAEN (Third Age Employment Network) (2005b) *The Pension Commission Interim Report, A briefing*, London: TAEN.

THES (Times Higher Education Supplement) (2005) 'Foundation degrees suffer 55 per cent dropout rates', 20 May 2005, p 11.

Treasury and Department for Work and Pensions (2003) *Full Employment in every region*, London: Stationery Office.

Tysome, T (2005) 'V-Cs end part-time students' raw deal', *Times Higher Education Supplement*, 22 April, p 7.

Williams, J and Kinnaird, R (2004) *National Survey of Adult Basic Skills in Wales*, prepared by the British Market Research Bureau for the Basic Skills Agency, http://www.basic-skills-wales.org.

Working Brief (2005a) issue 161, February, London: Centre for Social and Economic Inclusion.

Working Brief (2005b) issue 165, June, London: Centre for Social and Economic Inclusion.

Working Brief (2005c) issue 162, March, London: Centre for Social and Economic Inclusion.

Notes

1 Annual local area LFS data for 2003–04 are based on the largest-ever annual LFS sample of about 170,000 UK households consisting of around 390,000 people, of whom over 306,000 are aged 16 and over.

2 Social Grade A includes the upper and upper-middle classes and is generally grouped with Grade B, the middle classes. Grade C1 includes the lower-middle class, often called white-collar workers. Grade C2 mainly consists of skilled manual workers. Grade D comprises the semi-skilled and unskilled working class, and is usually linked with Grade E, those on the lowest levels of subsistence such as old age pensioners and those dependent upon welfare benefits.

3 It can be assumed that those answering this question are referring mainly to organised learning activities

4 This total includes both full-time and part-time students and students at further education colleges who were funded indirectly through an HEI. The latter have been counted within the numbers for that HEI. It excludes students studying on a directly funded HE programme at a FEC, and those studying at HE level in institutions that are not publicly funded.

5 Data returned by the Open University in 2003–04 provide a split between part-time first degree students and other undergraduate students. Previously, students taking OU credits were returned as studying at other undergraduate level or other postgraduate level, although the credits gained could count towards the award of a first degree or postgraduate degree. In 2003–04, OU students were reported according to their recorded award intention and the broad subject of that award intention at the HESA return date. However, OU students do not have to declare an award intention and many are still reported as studying for institutional credit within the 'combined' subject of study. This has had the affect of apparently reducing part-time other undergraduate numbers. It has also affected the number of records returned, as students who linked modules to two distinct qualification aims have been returned in two records. This change only affects enrolment data.

6 Classification based on that used in the 2001 census which replaced the social class indicator. The 'low' SEC indicator includes: small employers and own account workers, lower supervisory and technical occupations, routine and semi-routine occupations

7 Statistical First Release (SFR) 77 (*Destinations of leavers from higher education in the United Kingdom for the academic year 2002/03*) draws on the Destinations of Leavers from Higher Education (DLHE) record introduced in 2002–03, which replaced the previous First Destination Supplement (FDS). DLHE is a more comprehensive record which was expanded to cover leavers from part-time programmes and from additional postgraduate programmes. It covers what leavers are doing in relation to 'employment' and 'study'.

The statistics exclude those relating to qualifications obtained at FE colleges, the University of Buckingham and at other private and independent HE colleges.

8 For 2002–03 data, the category 'Assumed to be unemployed' includes those students who gave their employment circumstances as 'unemployed and looking for employment, further study or training' and who are also either in 'part-time study' or 'not in study', and those 'due to start a job within the next month' and who are also either in 'part-time study' or 'not in study'.

9 The Widening Participation Uplift is additional funds paid to the college usually for learners who are resident in postcodes deemed to be relatively disadvantaged or when the learning aim is basic skills.

10 Analysis by Ozan Jaquette of Oxford University.

11 Learndirect offers 'any time, any place, any pace' learning for individuals and businesses, with over 300 courses in three main portfolio areas: Skills for Life, ICT and Management. Learndirect centres are based in a wide range of venues, including public libraries, the high street, pubs and community centres (OECD, 2004b) .

12 Entry to Employment (E2E), which was rolled out nationally in August 2002, aims to prepare 'hard to reach' young people for entering apprenticeships, further education and jobs.

13 Respondents to the Labour Force Survey (LFS) who are of working age and not still at school or on college-based government training programmes are asked whether they received any job-related training or education in the previous four weeks and the previous 13 weeks.

14 The Employer Training Scheme provides employed adults who do not already have a full Level 2 qualification access to Skills for Life and Level 2 qualifications and information and advice through their employer. The service is aimed primarily at small and medium-sized organisations. After being piloted, it is being rolled out nationally and is part of the LSC's Level 2 Entitlement scheme in which eligible adults can qualify for fully funded Level 2 skills training.